# Health Education and Energy

# HEALTH EDUCATION AND ENERGY

*By*

**Dr. M. Lakshmi Narasaiah**
M.A., Ph.D.
*Professor of Economics,*
*Coordinator, Department of M.B.A.*
*Sri Krishnadevaraya University Post-graduate Centre,*
*Kurnool–518 002*
*Andhra Pradesh (India)*

DISCOVERY PUBLISHING HOUSE
NEW DELHI

**First Published–2005**

ISBN 81-7141-964-X



***Published by:***

**DISCOVERY PUBLISHING HOUSE**

4831/24, Prahlad Street, Ansari Road, Darya Ganj
New Delhi–110 002 (India)
*Phone: 23279245,* • *Fax: 91-11-23253475*
**e-mail: dphtemp@indiatimes.com**

**Printed at:**

Amit Enterprises, Delhi

# Preface

More than a third of the urban population in developing world live in housing of such poor quality with such inadequate provision for water, sanitation, drainage, garbage collection and health care that their health is constantly under threat. But, properly planned, cities can be safe and healthy.

In the cities of India, it is common for one child in three to die before the age of five and for virtually all infants, children and adults who survive to have disease burdens many times higher than they should.

Diarrhoea, tuberculosis and respiratory infections (each among the largest causes of death) are generally much increased by over-crowding, Many accidental injuries happen when there are three or more persons living in each small room in shelters made of flammable materials and there is little chance of providing occupants (especially children) with protection from open fires or stoves.

But cities also include some of the India's safest and most healthy neighbourhoods. High densities allow much lower costs for supplying each household with piped, treated water supplies and most forms of health, educational and emergency services.

Sanitation and drainage may be costly in cities, as complex systems are needed to cope with high densities and large population concentrations but city households can generally afford to pay more—and are prepared to do so if they get a good service.

Cities may be considered ecologically unsustainable because of high consumption and waste levels but well planned and managed cities can combine high living standards with remarkably low levels of energy consumption, resource use and wastes. The concentration of people and production creates many more possibilities of collecting and recycling wastes and for walking, bicycling and a high quality public transport.

For many, city-life is one of excessive workloads and drudgery, yet cities remain centre of culture—including the visual and decorative arts, music, dance, theatre and literature. Most cities have a large reserve of young people on whose initiative and energy they could draw to improve condition—yet most such people find that their cities offer them little hope and little prospect of employment. If cities have such potential to provide healthy, stimulating and valued places to live and work for all age groups, why do so achieve this?

**Supporting Change**

Much of the explanation is the lack of 'good governance'. Good governance in any city means encouragement and support from all levels of government for a great range of investments of capital, expertise and time by individuals, households, communities, voluntary organizations and NGOs—as well as private enterprises. In most cities in India, the total value of investments made by people in their own homes and neigbourhoods exceeds many times the total value of capital investments made by city and municipal authorities. Yet governments and aid agencies usually ignore (or deem illegal) most such efforts.

Most households who want their own home cannot afford to purchase one—or at least one that is legal. They cannot obtain housing loans so the cost of the house purchase can be spread over a number of years—as they cannot meet the (usually) inappropriate conditions set by banks or housing finance institutions. If they turn to building their own home—as most do—they have to occupy or purchase the site illegally. They often have to build on dangerous sites—in floodplains or on slopes with frequent landslides or mudslides—as the cost of safer sites is too high.

Even if they can qualify, for a housing loan; most such loans are for finished houses, not for incremental construction.

And even when they have developed their own home and neighbourhood into a viable residential area, governments usually refuse to provide these with roads water supplies, drains and other essential infrastructure, because they are 'illegal'.

What would cities look like today if governments had supported these individual and community efforts by ensuring that land, building materials, credit and technical advice were as cheap and readily available as possible? Or if government-community partnerships had been formed to, at least, improve water supply, sanitation, drainage and health care.

**Dr. M. Lakshmi Narasaiah**

# Contents

# 1

# The Environment, The Economy and Public Health:

*An integrated view*

The environment is central to the health of people and their economies. Just as a foetus is totally dependent on the life-support system of the mother during her pregnancy, so the health and vitality of people and their economies are totally dependent on their environments. Unfortunately, many people do not see it that way. They either see the environment as dependent on the economy—such as the politician who says: "let's make the economy strong, then we'll fix the environment when we can afford it"—or they see little connection between health and the environment, whether they are "deep greens" campaigning on ecological issues or doctors treating individual patients and individual illnesses. Whether we are politicians, greens or doctors, is there not a more efficient way to fulfil our aims? For this, a broader perspective is essential.

All economies are sub-systems of the larger environmental system which provides the:

- Sources of energy and materials;
- Sinks for pollution and other wastes;
- Services of water, nutrients and carbon recycling.
- Space for living, working and aesthetics ("a walk in the woods and the song of a bird")

Neglect of this life-support system of the "4 S's" leads to weaker or defunct economies as vegetation, food, soils, water or air become contaminated or exhausted and gradually fail to support economic activity. This is dramatically illustrated in the Aral Sea region, or the collapsed Canadian salmon fishing communities.

## Indirect Social Costs

Less catastrophic but still costly is where economic damage is caused by pesticides and nutrient contamination of groundwater, involving millions of Rupees in water treatment. This is a social cost to the economy that the agricultural sector does not include in the price of its food: an economic distortion that reduces the real wealth of society via false price signals that encourage the over-use of pesticides and fertilisers. Similarly, the "external" costs on society of road-respiratory-induced accidents, noise, respiratory and circulatory diseases and congestion amount to a lot of money to any government but these costs are not borne by transport users, which mean that transport is encouraged beyond the level that is economic for society as a whole. By internalising these externalities via taxes and other means, the market prices for transport would become fairer and more efficient. Currently only about 30% of transport externalities are covered by transport taxes. But if the health of an economy is dependent on the health of its environment, what about the health of its people?

Without access to the basics of clean water, shelter, fresh air and food, people obviously suffer. Even in more developed economies where the link between everyday life and the environment is not so visible, the role of environmental factors in disease and well-being is significant. Most of the major diseases such as heart disease, cancer, respiratory diseases and allergies have an environmental as well as a genetic component within a multi-factorial chain of causation. And while each environmental factor may be small, if the links in the chain of causation are inter-dependent, as they often appear to be then removing even a small link can break the chain.

## Environmental Factors

Take asthma in children, for example. These seem to be

many causes, from a child's genetic inheritance to its nutritional status, which in turn help determine how it reacts to the many environmental factors, both indoor (such as mites, pets, damp, environmental tobacco smoke, nitrogen oxides) and outdoor (such as pollen and pollution from industry and traffic), that have been implicated in asthma causation. Therefore it is clear that diagnoses of asthma and many other diseases should systematically embrace environmental factors. This will be a significant challenge for doctors whose time is scarce and whose training is not usually appropriate.

This multi-causal chain will vary in its exact make-up from child to child, but for children overall, even if the evironmental factors such as damp housing to traffic fumes may be less important than, say, genetic make-up or nutritional status, the environmental factors may be the ones that can be most cost effectively removed, thus breaking the causal chain. And, as with many environmental issues, there are secondary benefits of action, such as less noise or fewer accidents from traffic reduction, or energy savings from dry houses, which further justify the environmental actions even where exact causations are not well understood.

The environmental causes of disease and ill health are a controversial and ill understood area of science and opinions vary about their significance. Some say that, for Western Europe, perhaps 2-3% of public disease and ill-health is determined by known environmental factors but others maintain that it must be far more significant. They point to the sharp incense over the last two or three decades in asthma, allergies, and cancers (particularly of the reproductive organs such as breast and testicles) and related ill-health such as sperm count decline, which cannot be explained by genetic causes. They also observes that the large differences in health between the socio-economic classes cannot be explained without involving significant environmental causation.

It is thought that the ubiquitous presence of low doses of mixtures of chemicals in food, drink, air, consumer products and the general environment are playing some role in public ill health, even if the evidence for this is far from substantial.

**Impact on Public Health**

But what about environmental programmes and campaigns being little concerned with health? well, history so far shows that the environment only gets serious attention when it is seen to be damaging either the economy or public health. Yet because "everything connects" in "socio-enviro" systems, action to stop infectious diseases from water contamination, or to reduce skin cancer from ozone depletion, leads to a better environment for all speices. And if upland forests are preserved because they are seen to be cheaper and more effective water regulators (which reduce the risk of lowland flooding) than dams, then upland biodiversity benefits anyway, even if it was last in the queue for political attention.

Although public health may be seen by some as only a small part of "the environment", much environmental progress depends upon the political weight of the health impacts. For example, the cost benefit exercise on the current multi-pollutant/ effect programme on acidification, eutrophication and low-level ozone shows that it is the benefits to human health, not eco-system damage, that provide the main economic justification for further reductions in $SO_2$, $No_x$ and $NH_3$. Ecologists need the language of public health in order to maximise political support for the environment. So, it is out of our specialist "boxes" of economics, health and ecology, and into a shared systems approach, with integrated programmes that build partnerships for progress.

# 2

# Towards Healthy Cities

More than a third of the urban population in developing world live in housing of such poor quality with such inadequate provision for water, sanitation drainage, garbage collection and health care that their health is constantly under threat. But, properly planned, cities can be safe and healthy.

In the cities of India, it is common for one child in three to die before the age of five and for virtually all infants, children and adults who survive to have disease burdens many times higher than they should.

Diarrhoea, tuberculosis and respiratory infections (each among the largest causes of death) are generally much increased by over-crowding. Many accidental injuries happen when there are three or more persons living in each small room in shelters made of flammable materials and there is little chance of providing occupants (especially children) with protection from open fires or stoves.

But cities also include some of the India's safest and most healthy neighbourhoods. High densities allow much lower costs for supplying each household with piped, treated water supplies and most forms of health, educational and emergency services.

Sanitation and drainage may be costly in cities, as complex systems are needed to cope with high densities and large population concentrations but city households can generally afford to pay more—and are prepared to do so if they get a good service.

Cities may be considered ecologically unsustainable because of high consumption and waste levels but well planned and managed cities can combine high living standards with remarkably low levels of energy consumption, resource use and wastes. The concentration of people and production creates many more possibilities of collecting and recycling wastes and for walking, bicycling and a high quality public transport.

For many, city-life is one of excessive workloads and drudgery, yet cities remain centres of culture—including the visual and decorative arts, music, dance, theatre and literature. Most cities have a large reserve of young people on whose initiative and energy they could draw to improve condition—yet most such people find that their cities offer them little hope and little prospect of employment. If cities have such potential to provide healthy, stimulating and valued places to live and work for all age groups, why do so achieve this?

**Supporting Change**

Much of the explanation is the lack of 'good governance'. Good governance in any city means encouragement and support from all levels of government for a great range of investments of capital, expertise and time by individuals, households, communities, voluntary organizations and NGOs—as well as private enterprises. In most cities in India, the total value of investments made by people in their own homes and neighbourhoods exceeds many times the total value of capital investments made by city and municipal authorities. Yet governments and aid agencies usually ignore (or deem illegal) most such efforts.

Most households who want their own home cannot afford to purchase one—or at least one that is legal. They cannot obtain housing loans so the cost of the house purchase can be spread over a number of years—as they cannot meet the (usually) inappropriate conditions set by banks or housing finance institutions. If they turn to building their own home—as most do—they have to occupy or purchase the site illegally. They often have to build on dangerous sites—in floodplains or on slopes with frequent landslides or mudslides—as the cost of safer sites is too high.

Even if they can qualify, for a housing loan; most such loans are for finished houses, not for incremental construction. And even when they have developed their own home and neighbourhood into a viable residential area, governments usually refuse to provide these with roads water supplies, drains and other essential infrastructure, because they are 'illegal'.

What would cities look like today if governments had supported these individual and community efforts by ensuring that land, building materials, credit and technical advice were as cheap and readily available as possible? Or if government-community partnerships had been formed to, at least, improve water supply, sanitation, drainage and health care.

These work within what is often called the 'social economy'—the great variety of initiatives and actions that are organized and controlled locally and that are not profit-oriented. The social economy includes the work of citizen groups, residents' associations, street or barrio clubs, youth clubs, and parent associations that support local schools. It includes many voluntary groups that provide services for the elderly, the physically disabled or other individuals in need of social. It often includes many initiatives that make cities safer and more fun helping provide supervised play space, sport and recreational opportunities for children and youth. It may provide formal or informal supervision or maintenance of parks, squares, and other public spaces.

The social economy not only 'gets things done' but also creates a dense fabric of relationships that allows citizens to work together in identifying and acting on local problems. Its value to a 'healthy city' is enormous, even if it is often forgotten by governments and international agencies.

The capacity of city authorities to govern is not the same as the capacity to invest, since these authorities can do much to encourage and support the social economy. City authorities can often greatly increase the supply and reduce the cost of land for housing by changing inappropriate regulations, streamlining planning and land use control, procedure and making better use of publicly owned land.

City authorities should also have the main role in enforcing legislation on, air and water pollution and occupational health and safety. This does not require large investment by public authorities, but it can do much to improve health and the quality of life in a city. Good governance also means managing competing claims and finding common ground between enterprises, trade unions and residents about what should be done to make the city more healthy.

Achieving a healthy city needs a representative political system through which the priorities of citizens and businesses can influence policies and actions. Democratic structures remain among the best checks on the misallocation of resources by city and municipal governments. Actively involving a wide range of local groups in developing 'city governance' helps ensure that the different priorities of a wide range of groups are addressed.

The key issue is not so much identifying what should be done to achieve more healthy cities. This is well known. It is identifying how it should be done, especially how governments and international agencies can support a vast range of activities by individuals, households and communities that help build and maintain healthy cities—which to date they have ignored or even (for many governments) repressed.

# 3

# Health Care Relief in Conflict Situations:

## *What Can We Learn from the Food Relief Experience?*

Conflicts and war occur in many of the poorest nations where populations already suffer from severe ill health. War leads to an increase in disease and to a worsening of the already fragile condition of populations. Health care itself becomes a victim of conflict. Many deaths which occur during these emergencies are not discretely related to the conflict itself but are the result of lacking access to public health services. Furthermore, conflict itself but are the result of lacking access to public health services. Furthermore, conflict contributes to the deterioration of already pre-existing structural weaknesses of the health care system. An example is the period of internal conflict in Uganda (1970-1986) when health services declined in the aftermath of the war due to the impact of foreign assistance and the planning vacuum in which the activities took place.

### The Impact of Conflict on Health Care

Conflict and civil strife may lead to a major disruption of health services. This is not only a result of physical destruction but also of finding shortages since national governments increase spending on military activities. Casualties increase the demand for curative services, which can divert already limited resources from preventive care.

In the case of the Sudanese civil war a large majority of health professionals was forced to abandon rural health professionals was forced to abandon rural health services and left for urban areas or neighbouring countries in order to find new employment. Entire preventive health services such as immunisation as well as water and sanitation projects collapsed leaving the population exposed to infectious diseases and epidemics. In urban areas, the gap in public health care provision is sometimes filled with the expansion of private services. In rural areas, private sector involvement in health care is rather marginal, apart from some omission hospitals or pharmacies. Therefore the non-formal health care sector often makes a substantial contribution towards health care.

With the rise of internal conflicts in Africa, more people suffer from emergency situations. This also increases the influence and impact of international donors. External assistance nowadays accounts for more than 25 per cent of government health expenditure in sub-Saharan Africa.

The size of donor involvement reflects the power of international agencies to control the policy domain. Countries in conflict or post-conflict situations are under pressure to 'rescue' their health systems and accept global policies in exchange for aid assistance and relief.

However, in the period after 1991, donor organisations tended to increase their expenditures for high profile humanitarian operations rather than ordinary development activities. This shift may reflect the increasing influence of media covering some of the conflicts. Too often, organisations intervene with ad hoc assistance without sufficient consultation at local level.

## Donors' Perceptions in Designing Relief Interventions

Today, in many parts of sub-Saharan Africa development assistance has virtually collapsed and has been substituted by relief assistance. The problem is that relief intervention are based on a Western construction of reality, reflecting what is desirable and necessary in times of conflict. Most interventions therefore stress physical and material needs, presuming that the social aspect of food and health is not an immediate issue to address.

The question which arises here is on who's views and perceptions these needs are based? While donors interest may be guided from the perspective of ill-health, the recipient government may be concerned with the collapse of the economy. However, any intervention needs to take into account that local knowledge and practices are shaped by state interests as well as power relationships. The common belief that health care systems always collapse due to conflict is sometimes mistaken. Considering the fact that today's internal conflicts are often fragmented, conflicts do not necessarily result in a breakdown of the health care delivery system.

Donors tend to respond with a 'package approach and developing countries ministries of health increasingly play a symbolic role. The evidence suggests that international organisations tend to create vertical programmes, which undermine national public health programmes. Foreign interventions are technically sophisticated and reorienting health are towards a more curative approach. Too little attention given to strengthen the health care system within its own limits, providing more appropriate technology, drugs and emphasizing the training of local health staff.

Another vital issue concerns the existence of already fragile health information systems. Agencies tend to bring their own systems which leads to further fragmentation. The local perspective on what are the 'basic needs' in physical and social health are usually not considered. Health relief interventions do not recognize the potential of the communities and the non-formal health sector such as healers and traditional midwifes in supporting and maintaining health care sector presents a substantial contribution towards health. It is not the question between choosing either allopathic or traditional services, it is more the decision which kind of illness will be best treated by which practitioner. There is a need in further exploring the role of this sector particularly since this is sometimes the only service available for certain populations.

## Responding to Local Needs

More community-based public health interventions could be vital to reduce mortality and morbidity. For example in Somalia during the 1992 war and famine high mortality rates due to measles and diarrhoea could have been prevented by involving the communities in primary health care activities such as immunisation and nutrition improvement.

In the African context Tigray is an example where health services had been sustained and partially expanded during the civil war against the Ethiopian government. Local government structures called baitos promoting social and economic development. Baitos encouraged communities to establish revolving funds for drugs and medical equipment. It actually functioned as an early type of community financing system.

As mentioned above, the challenge in changing health care relief strategies is to overcome the approach of short-term interventions, particularly in changing conflict environment where conflicts are complex and interruptions are no longer short-term.

Therefore interventions need to be linked with the process of conflict resolution to avoid health care or food aid being used by politically dominant groups.

**Food Relief in Conflict Situations**

Food interventions have both a survival and a production function. For example, food-for-work may be part of an income programme or food aid can be monetised to generate local currency. However, food aids have to be seen beyond the objective to fulfill nutritional goals, it also defines relationships between social groups in regard to food accessibility and how food is shared. Food aid is aiming to meet people's basic food requirements and minimising risk and severity of disease by complementing services such as basic health care.

In more stable political conditions where free food aid is given it presents an income transfer by releasing income, which normally is spent on food. However, in conflict situations food relief frequently becomes part of the dynamics of conflict such in the case of Sudan where it is used to sustain the struggle between the North and the South without resolving it. Furthermore, the military attack food supplies in the fight against rebels who depend on the support from the communities.

Health is also a matter of food security. When food insecurity coincides with conflict situations, health and survival are threatened. Food security provides some concepts on how and why vulnerable households manage to survive in periods of hardship (coping strategies).

**Coping Strategies in African Trouble Zones**

Today, most conflicts in Africa such as the ones in the Great Lake Region, Angola or Congo cause major problems of food insecurity. They are linked to the civil wars which produce substantial social disruption as a result of massive population movements. The analysis of coping strategies showed that household respond to these conflict situations by eating less, selling livestock and land, or trying to find new sources of income.

In some emergency situations, however such coping mechanisms may fall. In the case of the war in Mozambique food aid was vital since coping strategies were limited and people had to sell all their assets, which was particular, true for internationally displaced persons and refugees.

It has been argued that food relief bypasses local structures in favour of those qualifying on a nutrition status criterion, decided by international organisations, or it may attract populations to refugee camps to receive free food rations and thereby undermines local production. In the case of Rwanda food aid was targeted at the internally displaced and left out the local population. This can be due to donor bias in needs assessment.

Food scarcity is not always so result of civil war but its creation may be rather a political objective. An example is food relief manipulated by local elites and the military like in the case of Sudan. It can be summarised that generally relief operations often bear the risk of fueling the process of instability and violence rather that helping to contain the situation.

**Lessons from Food Relief for the Health Sector?**

Through the experience of food relief in recent civil wars such as Sudan, Somalia, Mozambique etc., there has been an increasing awareness of the economic and political context in which operations take place. Like food relief, health care is a political tool, which can, if not properly targeted, undermine peoples access to health care services. While food production is linked to food security, it is more difficult to identify factors leading to self-sufficiency in health care.

As mentioned above, food aid is aiming to insure survival. It also has an economic aspect, protecting household assets. Health care relief is targeted to assure immediate physical survival based on the importance of social health. Unfortunately, curative interventions hardly consider the socio-cultural dimension of health. Therefore it would be beneficial if health care interventions consider local norms and traditions. Interventions should be compatible and complement local health programmes. The emphasis should be on strengthening formal and non-formal health institutions both in service provision and training.

In food relief, distribution and needs assessment identification are controversial issues for discussion. While the programme design is shaped by donor's perceptions, the actual programmes are influenced by the priorities of some powerful leaders as well as the socio-economic and political context.

Health care interventions need to analyse these issues in the context of economic and political systems in order to identify the most vulnerable groups, for example populations living in areas which are more, operations require a stronger involvement of communities both as users and active participants carry out and maintain public health programmes.

There is a need for a new concept to be designed, which applies, to chronic emergencies. In the absence of a policy framework, guidelines need to be developed in order to overcome the inconsistency in planning and implementation. Donors need to change their assumptions on which they plan their health relief responses. A starting point in improving the efficiency of these operations is to provide institutional support to local authorities and organisations and involve them in the planning and implementation of programmes.

# 4

# Children's Health and the Environment

Children today live in an environment vastly different from that of a few generations ago. Economic development, increased urbanisation and the consequences of war in many countries have added to the traditional environmental hazards, those problems associated with environmental pollution. Thus, while some traditional children' diseases such as diarrhoea, malnutrition and infectious diseases persist in many countries, environmentally-related illnesses such as asthma, respiratory illnesses due to environmental tobacco smoke (ETS), as well as mortality and morbidity due to injuries, are increasing. In childhood cancer in some countries and the potential risks of endocrine-disrupting chemicals are among the emerging health threats that need careful vigilance. Children of lower socio-economic status are likely to suffer disproportionately from all these health threats as a consequence of living in highly polluted environments, poor quality housing, lower levels of education, and of restricted access to environmental and health care services.

## Children's Vulnerability

The concern for children's vulnerability to environmental health threats is based on several factors. Children receive greater exposures than adults do because they drink more water, eat more food and have higher breathing rates per unit of body weight. Because they are undergoing rapid growth and development, toxicant effects at specific times may have irreversible consequences. For example, if vital connections between nerve cells fail to form during brain development, there is high risk that the resulting neurobehavioural dysfunction will be permanent and irreversible. Also, because most children have more future year of life than adults, they have more time to develop any chronic disease that may be triggered by early environmental exposures.

## Public Health Threats

Asthma, injuries, and the effects of environmental tobacco smoke (ETS) are among the most significant public health threats to children. Childhood asthma is increasingly prevalent in allmost all countries. What causes asthma is not known, but several environmental factors, such as indoor air quality (particularly exposure to the house-dust mite) and ETS, have been linked with the increase in asthma. In addition, outdoor air pollutants such as particulates, sulphur dioxide and ozone can exacerbate asthma symptoms. ETS, especially smoking by the mother, is a known risk factor for asthma. ETS is also known to cause acute and chronic middle ear disease and is associated with sudden infant death syndrome (SIDS).

## Potential for Prevention

The variation in asthma and injury rates and the evidence of the role of certain environmental factors underline the potential for prevention. Public policies should seek to avoid preventable childhood diseases by preventing exposures to environmental agents and considering children's characteristics and susceptibilities in the development of environmental health legislation. Promoting citizen awareness and participation in policy-making through education and access to environmental information are important elements in achieving a safe environment for children. In this context, children are not only consumers with rights, but also citizens who can play an active role towards their own protection.

## International Awareness

Several international agreements have acknowledged children's vulnerabilities and have committed their signatories to protect children's health from the effects of a deteriorating environment. This year, many countries will address several of the environmental health threats to children through international and national action. It is expected that a large international collaborative initiative will result under the guidance of WHO and other international organisation.

# 5

# Climate Change and Human Health

Changes in the India's climate, stemming from the greenhouse effect, are highly likely to damage human health. Food and fresh water supplies will be disrupted, millions of people displaced, and disease patterns altered dangerously and unpredictably.

Human health could be affected by even quite small changes in average mean temperature, and there is the prospect of some major diseases flourishing in warmer conditions and of more resistant strains of infection emerging.

The population in India most vulnerable to the negative impacts of global warming are in the lower-income groups, residents of coastal lowlands and islands, those living in semi-arid lands, and the urban poor in the squatter settlements, slums and shanty-towns of large cities.

Present strategies for immunization, coping with disease vectors or carriers, providing safe drinking water, and improving nutrition are all based on existing climate regimes, ecosystems, and sea and solar radiation level. These are all expected to change, but exactly how much cannot be preducted. It is therefore, virtually impossible to adjust health and nutritional strategies to take account of possible climate changes.

Humans can adapt to moderate changes in temperature and to occasional extremes. But this adaptive capacity is relatively low in infants and the elderly; it rises through childhood and adolescence to reach a maximum which can be maintained up to about 30 years of age.

A changing climate would after the ecosystems of the vectors or agents which carry or cause many diseases, whether these be viruses, bacteria, parasites, plants, insects or other animals such as mosquitoes and snails. As the weather warms, the boundaries of the tropics may extend into the present subtropics, and parts of temperate areas may become subtropical. As air temperatures increase, some diseases will become common in regions which once rarely knew them and where there is little natural resistance to them. As result, death rates may also climb significantly.

It is possible that warmer weather around the world will cause increases in summer diseases and decreases in those associated with winter. Diseases contracted from both water and air will also spread more readily as ambient temperatures rise. In a warmer climate, mosquitoes and other vectors also may migrate vertically, up into highlands which were once too cold for them. This may be particularly hazardous in tropical highland areas where there is no natural resistance to malaiara.

Changes in temperature, rainfall, humidity and storm patterns may affect diseases borne by vectors in two ways. First, they will directly affect the vector's reproduction rate, biting rate, and the duration and frequency of human exposure. Second, they may modify agricultural systems or plant species, thus changing the relationship between host and vector. Developments rates of malarial mosquitoes, for example, increase with warmer temperatures, but these pests need wet areas in which to breed.

Sea-level rise could also spread infectious disease by flooding sewerage and sanitation systems in coastal cities, and increase the incidence of diarrhoea in children. The flooding of hazardous waste dumps and sanitation systems could lead to long-term contamination of crop lands.

Rising seas may also disrupt marine habitats land aquatic food chains. Since fish constitute 40 per cent of all animal protein consumed by the people of India such a disruption of the marine ecosystem would affect the food supplies of many millions of people and dramatically increase protein deficiency and malnutrition. Changes in the availability of food and water, as well as radical shifts in disease patterns, could initiate large migrations of people, exacerbating food shortages, overcrowding, social stress and instability.

Some of the factors contributing significantly to global warming, such as the burning of fossil fuels and the use of chlorofluorocarbons (CFCs) and halons, threaten human health in other ways too. A typical petrol-driven motor car, for example, emits carbon monoxide, sulphur and nitrogen oxides, hydrocarbons, low-level ozone and lead-all of which are hazardous to health.

The ozone-depleting CFCs and halons pose a particular threat to humans through an increased rising of skin cancer, cataracts and lower immunity to other illnesses as a result of increased exposure to ultraviolet B radiation from the sun. Skin cancer risks are expected to rise most among fair-skinned.

# 6

## Taking Poverty to Heart:

### *Non-Communicable Diseases and the Poor*

Non-Communicable Diseases (NCDs) are the leading cause of death worldwide. Their emergence as the predominant health problem in wealthy countries accompanied economic development. As a result, NCDs are often referred to as 'diseases of affluence'. But is this a misleading term? It suggests that these are not major problems for the world's poor, which is quite simply wrong, as this article illustrates. Is it time to rethink policy on NCDs?

NCDs include cardiovascular disease (CVD), such as stroke and heart attack, diabetes, chronic lung disease, cancer, diseases of bones and joints, and mental illness. The single biggest killer is coronary heart disease, followed by other CVDs, cancer and chronic lung disease. Diabetes is a major contributor to deaths form CVD, but also causes its own unique complications. Common risk factors for these conditions include smoking, physical activity, obesity and diets high in saturated fat and sodium and lwo in fruit and vegetables.

By 2020, NDCs will be the biggest cause of death in all regions apart from sub-Saharan Africa. It is predicted that in 2010, the number of people with diabetes worldwide will be double the level in 1995 and that the biggest increase (both proportionately and in absolute number) will be in poorer regions. CVD occurs at an earlier age in developing countries, increasing the potential adverse economic and social consequences.

NCDs are already major health problems for adults in the poorest countries of the world. Demographic data show that age-specific death rates from NCDs in Tanzania are higher than in wealthier countries. Mortality rates for some NCDs, such as stroke, are particularly high. However, while NCDs account for 80 per cent of adult deaths in developed regions, the figure is less than 30 per cent in Tanzania, reflecting the continuing burden of infectious disease. Countries like Tanzania suffer The worst of both worlds'. Even within a country, 'diseases of affluence' is a misleading term. A more accurate label is 'diseases of Urbanisation'. Several studies from developing countries show increased levels of high blood pressure and other NCD risk factors in urban compared to rural populations. Even within urban areas, the more affluent do not always suffer the greatest burden.

The rise of NCDs in developing countries is inextricably linked to economic and cultural globalisation. This is exemplified by the activities of multinational tobacco companies. Tobacco-related deaths will exceed the toll due to HIV and become the single largest preventable cause of death by 2020. Curbing the effects of globalisation on the prevention and treatment of NCDs will also require regulation of food and agriculture multinationals and the pharmaceutical and healthcare industries.

Much of the projected rise in NCDs is preventable, particularly that due to smoking, poor diet, physical inactivity and obesity. Early action in some populations could prevent the emergence of these risk factors altogether; in other, the challenge is to reduce established levels. Although it is unclear whether all major risk factors are equally important in every region, the strength and consistency of data on the core risk factors in several ethnic groups justify preventative action now.

Lessons from risk factor intervention studies in rich and middle income countries suggest that success requires.

- Broad intersectoral action
- Community participation
- Appropriate legislation

- Involvement of appropriate NGOs
- Health services changes—to manage those at high risk and promote public education.

Even apparently minor changes, such as a small fall in average population blood pressure, can have substantial benefits. However, some preventative pogrammes have produced disappointing results and almost all have failed to halt the ubiquitous increase in obesity. This highlights the difficulty of promoting healthy behaviour by individuals who are surrounded by barriers to change and inducements to lead an unhealthy lifestyle.

Health systems in developing countries face both a growing need for prevention programmes and increasing numbers of individuals requiring treatment. The complications of high blood pressure and diabetes can be reduced by the delivery of effective healthcare. Crucially, this entails:

- Partnership between patients and health professionals with the knowledge, ability and resources to take appropriate measures over many years.
- Cheap and effective drugs and the implementation of simple treatment protocols, as promoted by WHO and the CVD initiative of the Global Forum for Health Research.

An appropriate policy strategic framework is essential for such initiatives to be effective on a large scale. Even in the poorest countries people are already seeking healthcare for NCDs in both the public and private sectors, particularly in urban areas. Whatever the balance of priorities between different conditions, existing resources should be used as effectively as possible. Rapid evaluation methods can provide policy-makers with information on the current levels and quality of care and identify the main opportunities for improving health services.

The proper planning and co-ordination of NCD prevention and treatment, whether globally or nationally, requires up-to-date data on risk factor and disease levels—currently missing for much of the world. To address this lack, the WHO Non-

Communicable Disease and Mental Health Surveillance section is promoting a standardised approach to enable comparisons across regions and over time, preparing the first ever 'world risk status' report for the major NCDs. This will provide a truly global perspective on the size and nature of the problem.

As this article has shown, NCDs are major health problems even in the world's poorest countries, including those regions where infectious diseases continue to take a huge toll. The NCD burden will grow substantially in low land middle-income countries over the next 10 to 20 years. NCDs will increasingly demand attention and require the right balance between competing priorities for prevention, cure and care. In meeting this challenge, national policy-makers will need to follow the lead of WHO and develop a strategic framework that plans for surveillance, prevention and appropriate health sector reforms.

# 7

# Why Don't We Stop Tuberculosis?

Tuberculosis, a disease many people associate with sequestered sanatoriums that were long ago abandoned or razed, has now reemerged as the number one killer among the infectious or communicable diseases. The current TB epidemic is expected to grow worse, especially in India, because of the evolution of multi-drug-resistant strains and the emergence of AIDS, which compromises human immune systems and make them more susceptible to infectious diseases.

The resurgence of tuberculosis comes at a time when other infectious diseases that were once thought to be well-controlled—malaria and cholera, among them—have increased and new diseases, notably AIDS, have emerged. Despite the advances in modern medicine, infectious diseases have persisted and continue to have a major effect on public health; in the 50 years following the discovery of antibiotics, efforts to control age-old epidemics have been overcome not by a lack of medical knowledge but by structural problems, including the lack of adequate health care in many parts of India, and increased rates of travel and migration.

Tuberculosis has special characteristics that set it apart form other infectious diseases most of which rely on mosquitoes, rats, or water to transmit infection. Tubercle bacilli only live in human tissues, and tuberculosis can only be transmitted by close contact with an infected person. In a healthy individual, the immune system is normally able to wall off and isolate the bacilli in a nodule. This essentially neutralizes the tubercle bacillus, so the person has what is referred to as an inert infection. If the immune system remains strong, there is only a 5 to 10 per cent chance of developing TB from an inert infection. But if the immune system is under severe stress—from HIV, diabetes, or chemotherapy for cancer, for example—the chances that the infection will develop into disease increase to as much as 10 per cent in a single year.

A person who has active TB can spread the infection simply by coughing, sneezing, singing, or even talking. Another person has only to inhale the bacilli to become infected. If the infection is not detected and treated promptly, one person with active tuberculosis can infect an average of 10 to 14 people in one year and sometimes many more.

Inert TB infections may show no symptoms at all. Only if those infections are activated will these people be at risk of developing the disease and transmitting it to others. Unfortunately, little is known about what activates a latent TB infection beyond the fact that people with healthy immune systems run a low risk of developing an active case of TB.

Because the already poor and disenfranchised Indian population carry a disproportionate burden of tuberculosis, the disease has a certain stigma attached to it. But the unsanitary and crowded living conditions that are often connected to poverty do not cause TB to spread; they increase the chances that the infection will spread from person to person and the chances that a person's immune system may already be weak and therefore less able to fight the infection. Despite the misconceptions, tuberculosis is exacerbated only by the failure to detect and treat the infection properly and by close contact with infected individuals.

More than 95 per cent of TB cases reported in 1995 were in the developing world, an estimated two-thirds of them in Asia. India accounted for 2.1 million cases. India is with a disproportionate number of cases because AIDS is spreading quickly, health services are inadequate, and little money is available for treatment.

To identify and diagnose TB must be combined with sufficient infrastructure and resources, such as vaccines, medicines, trained health personnel, and clinics. As with other diseases, funding for research and prevention and treatment programmes is essential. Thanks to modern medicine, there is a low-cost, effective TB treatment with high cure rates among infected adult. But if patients don't take the drugs consistently or don't complete treatment, TB strains develop that are more resistant to medicine, and sometimes even untreatable. If this drug regimen were used throughout India. It would reduce the rate of transmission and cut the number of deaths by half over the next 10 years.

The growing TB epidemic is a classic case of a public health crisis in India that could be headed off easily and inexpensively. Its fate will largely depend on the willingness of government and public health officials to invest up front in prevention and early intervention. If we ignore the extraordinary opportunity that exists now to fight the epidemic, we will pay a high price in lives and extensive health care costs later.

# 8

# Safe Motherhood is a Human Rights Issue

The death of a woman during pregnancy or childbirth is not only an health issue but also a matter of social injustice. Of the human rights currently acknowledged in national constitutions and in regional and international human rights treaties, many can be applied to safe motherhood. Many such treaties and conventions are based on the 1948 Declaration of Human Rights (1); they include the Convention on the Elimination of All forms of Discrimination against Women (2), the Convention on the Rights of the Child (3) the European Convention for the Protection of Human Rights and Fundamental Freedom (4), the American Convention on Human Rights (5) and the African Charter on Human and Peoples' Rights (6).

Human rights of relevance to safe motherhood can be grouped into the following four principal categories.

- **Rights relating to life, liberty and security of the person,** which require governments to ensure both accesses to appropriate health care during pregnancy and childbirth, and women's rights to decide whether, when, and how often to bear children. Governments must therefore address factors within the economic, legal, social, and health systems that deny women these fundamental rights.

- **Rights relating to the foundation of families and of family life,** which require governments to provide access to health-services and other facilities that women need to establish families and to enjoy life within a family.

- **Rights relating to health care and the benefits of scientific progress, including health information and education,** which require governments to provide access to good sexual and reproductive health care with appropriate referral systems. The measures needed to ensure safe motherhood can be provided through primary health care irrespective of a country's level of economic development. Central to these rights is information on a range of reproductive health issues, including family planning, abortion, and sex education.
- **Rights relating to equality and nondiscrimination,** which require governments to provide access to services such as education and health care without discriminatory grounds such as sex, marital status, age, and socioeconomic class. Discriminatory policies include requirements for a woman to obtain the consent of her husband for particular health care interventions, requirements for parental authorization which have a differential impact on girls, and laws that criminalize medical procedures that only women need. Governments are in violation of their obligations when they fail to implement laws that effectively protect women's interests or to allocate health resources to meet women's particular need for safe pregnancy and childbirth.

The actions that governments need to take to promote safe motherhood as a human right fall into three groups.

- **Reform of laws** that prevent women from attaining the highest possible levels of health and nutrition needed for safe pregnancy and childbirth and that inhibit access to reproductive health information and services such as laws requiring women in need of health care to seek the authorization of husbands or other family members first.
- **Implemention of laws** that foster women's rights to good health and nutrition and that protect women's health interests such as laws that prohibit child marriage, female genital mutilation, rape, and sexual

abuse. Every effort should be made to implement laws that encourage the healthy timing of births, such as those that support the ecucation of girls, set a minimum age for marriage, and ensure women's access to essential health care.

- **Application of human right** in national legislation and policy to advance safe motherhood.

# 9

# Action for Safe Motherhood

Countries vary enormously in terms of the situations and challenges they face and their capacity to address these. However, experience from around the world over the past decade has demonstrated that a number of features are common to successful efforts to address maternal mortality. Reducing maternal mortality requires coordinated, long-term efforts. Actions are needed within families and communities, in society as a whole, in health systems, and at the level of national legislation and policy. Further, interactions among the interventions in these areas are critical to reducing maternal mortality and to building and supporting momentum for change.

## Legislative and Policy Actions

Changes in legislation and policy are essential to ensure safe motherhood. Long-term political commitment is an essential prerequisite. When decision-makers at the highest levels are resolved to address maternal mortality, the resources needed will be mobilized and the essential policy decisions will be taken. Without this level of commitment over the long term, projects cannot become programmes and activities cannot be sustained.

A supportive social, economic, and legislative environment allows women to overcome the various obstacles that limit their access to health care, such as distance from their homes to appropriate health facilities, lack of transport and, more critically, financial and social barriers. Proper maternal health care is limited when women have to pay for services and essential drugs, and when they must bear substantial hidden costs such as time lost for housework, paid employment, food production, and child care. Legislation that supports women's access to care must be formulated to permit health workers at the periphery of the health system to perform specific life-saving functions. Failing this, only highly skilled health professionals, based largely in urban centres, can provide such care, and only women with sufficient money and the means to reach such centres can benefit from it.

With these objectives, careful review of national laws and policies is necessary, particularly in the following areas:

- **Family planning.** Statutes that restrict women's access to family planning services (e.g. by requiring that a woman be married or that she should have her husband's approval) should be repealed. Policies must ensure that all couples and individuals have access to good-quality, voluntary, client-oriented, and confidential family planning information and to services that offer a wide choice of effective contraceptive methods. Policies should address regulatory, social, economic, and cultural factors that limit women's control over sexuality and reproduction, in order that pregnancies that are too early, too late, or too frequent may be avoided.
- **Adolescents and children.** Polices and programmes should encouage later marriage and childbearing and an expansion of the economic and educational opportunities for girls and women. Promotion of good nutrition in childhood and adolescence, as well as supplementation if necessary during pregnancy, provides protection for both women and their future children. Policies should also enable adolescents to take responsibility for and protect their sexual and reproductive health, and facilitate their access to health information and services. All children, before they reach the age at which they become sexually active, need to be taught the risks of unprotected sex and helped to develop the skills needed to protect themselves from sexual coercion.

- **Barriers to access.** Assigning health workers trained in midwifery to village-based health facilities can help over-come problems of distance and transport. Health workers should also be trained to deal sympathetically with women patients. Policies should support provision of services at minimum cost, at the same time, health worker should have job security, be paid adequate wages, and be provided with sufficient supplies to do their jobs. Policies that will increase women's decision-making power, particularly in regard to their own health, also essential.

- **Regulation of practice.** Protocols and statutes aimed at providing both routine maternal care and referral facilities for obstetric complications at each level of the health system need to developed. Responsibilities at each level for supervision, deployment of health care personnel, remuneration, and reporting procedures must be defined nationally. Development and promotion of education and training curricula are important, as is the setting of national norms and standards to govern the selection of trainees, trainers, and supervisors.

- **Delegation of authority.** Services should be decentralized so that facilities are available as close to people's homes as possible. Adequate supplies and equipment and trained staff should be available in all health facilities, particularly in rural and remote areas, together with written policies and protocols to guide service provision and to allow certain functions to be delegated to personnel at lower levels (when appropriately trained).

- **Abortion.** Availability of services for management of abortion complications and post-abortion care should be ensured by appropriate legislation. Where abortion is not prohibited by law, facilities for the safe termination of pregnancy should be made available. National policy can discourage unsafe abortion practices by promoting protection against unwanted pregnancy, and national helath campaigns to publicize the risks of unsafe abortion and the need to recognize and seek treatment for abortion complications.

# 10

## What is Known About Reducing Maternal Mortality?

Historical records demonstrate the significant improvements that can be achieved when key interventions are in place. Reductions in maternal mortality took place in Sweden during the 1800s, for example, as a result of a national policy favouring professional midwifery care for all births, coupled with establishment of standards for quality of care. By the beginning of the 20th century, maternal mortality in Sweden was the lowest around 230 per 1,00,000 live births compared with over 500 per 1,00,000 in the mid-1880s. In Denmark, Japan, Netherlands, and Norway, similar strategies produced comparable results. In England and Wales, significant reductions in maternal mortality were not apparent until the 1930s; at the national level, political commitment to the strategy was achieved only slowly and the introduction of professional midwifery was correspondingly delayed. In every case, however, the key to these improvements was the institution of fully professional maternity care.

In the USA, where strategy focused on hospital delivery by doctors, maternal mortality remained high because it proved difficult to establish adequate regulatory frameworks and mechanisms to ensure quality of care. In 1930, the maternal mortality ratio in the USA was still 700 per. 1,00,000 live births compared with 430 in England and Wales.

More recently, India witnessed significant reductions in maternal mortality in a relatively short period. From a level of over 1500 per 1,00,000 live births in 1940-1945, maternal mortality fell to 555 per 1,00,000 in 1950-1955, 239 per 1,00,000 within 10 years. And 95 per 1,00,000 by 1980. The figure is now 30 per 1,00,000. These improvements followed the introduction of a system of health facilities around the country allied to an expansion of midwifery skills and the spread of family planning. During the 1950s most births in India took place at home with the assistance of untrained birth attendants. By the end of the 1980s over 85% of all birth were attended by trained personnel.

Similar evidence of the effectiveness of health care interventions is available from China, Cuba, and Malaysia. These countries established community-based maternal health care systems comprising prenatal, delivery, and postpartum care and a system of referral to a higher level of care in the event of obstetric complications.

What these examples clearly demonstrate is that a country's overall economic wealth is not in itself the most important determinant of maternal mortality. There are numerous other examples of countries with modest levels of GNP which have achieved low maternal mortality.

# 11

# AIDS and the Responsibility of the Media

HIV/AIDS is one of the most terrible diseases the world has ever known. Estimates are that 37 million people worldwide are already infected with the deadly virus which weakens the human immunity system and leaves the body unprotected for the onslaught of a host of other diseases. So far, there is no vaccine to shield people against, HIV and there is no effective cure for the disease. This means that people inevitably die once they have caught the virus although some ten years or more may pass before the actual outbreak of AIDS in its final stages. UN figures say that 23 million of HIV/AIDS infected people live in sub-Saharan Africa alone—and all of them are doomed to die a painful death. At least 4 million newly infected were added to that number every year. As a result of the epidemic, life expectancy on the continent, which had been climbing persistently during the first three decades of post-independence development, will drop by ten years and more in many countries, especially in Southern Africa. And it will be the young, economically active people—who are also the sexually most active ones—that will be prominent among the victims. AIDS thus is not only a humanitarian disaster, it is also threatening to become another source of economic retardation and backwardness.

Why then there is still so little attention paid to the looming cirsis? Why are African leaders not getting together to discuss what needs to be done to control the situation? Why are they not using every means at their disposal to hammer the message home to their people. AIDS can be reigned in through more responsible behaviour and a change in sexual practices?

In Europe and America, when AIDS surfaced as a common threat in the late 1980s, every effort was made to alarm the public and especially the most vulnerable groups homosexuals, sex workers, people with frequently changing sex partners—about the dangers of unprotected sex. It was especially through the media that the almost everybody became aware of the AIDS menace. Prominent individuals—film stars, popmusicians, artists—who had been infected with AIDS outed themselves in the media and used their fame in anti-AIDS campaigns. Existing taboos on sexual practices were deliberately broken, and safer sex became a publicly debated issue. Much emphasis was placed on using condoms as a cheap and simple, but usually effective means to avoid infection. As a result of the public awareness campaigns and the continuous media coverage, new HIV infections in industrial countries returned to a relatively low level, and the disease today is considered to be under control, even though no medical cure has yet been found to treat AIDS patients.

While these successes were achieved in developed countries, the disease has been spreading with increasing speed in Africa and, lately, in Asia. Here, the society has reacted with far less openness to the challenges posed by AIDS. For a long time, political leaders and the media negated the menace in the erroneous belief that AIDS was mainly a disease of the decadent West. When they woke up to fact that AIDS was a problem not only for homosexuals in Los Angeles, London, or Berlin but also for "normal" hetero-sexual men and women in Uganda, South Africa or India, sexual taboos and religious inhibitions as well as social customs and attitudes proved powerful obstacles to launching publicity campaigns on the model of the Western countries.

As a result, there is still far too little information in developing countries on AIDS as a disease and what people can do to protect themselves against it. A recent study published by Johns Hopkins university in the United States, for instance, shows that only between 5 and 33 per cent of unmarried men are using condoms in sexual intercourse to avoid infection with AIDS. With women, condoms are even less known or popular than with men. The study says that the number of couples using condoms regularly is still very low worldwide. Instead of the 6 to 9 billion condoms used at present, 24 billions are required to control new infections. This is a question of money, because many of the people who ought to use condoms are among the poorest groups in breaking down barriers created out of prejudice and ingrained sexual behaviour.

Here, the media have a vital role to play. It is not enough to put up a few posters in town which warn against AIDS. The message has to be direct and concrete—Mechal in Thailand has shown how a witty and effective pro-condom campaign can be conducted even in a country with a strong Buddhist tradition—and it should not shy away from breaking sexual taboos. Equally important all media should be used—newspapers, radio, TV. Films, video—to carry the message. AIDS awareness should always be part of reproductive health information, and needed, both are part of the same coin if more condoms are used to prevent unwanted pregnancies, a welcome side-effect will be a reduction in new HIV infections.

AIDS and the menace it poses to the survival of large parts of African and Asian populations is not a pleasant subject. But it will not go away by keeping silent about its threat. Political leaders and the media must make it a topic for urgent action. And the people must change their sexual habits and behaviour and opt for safer sex. Otherwise, the future of whole regions on this globe will be grim.

# 12

# Energy and Sustainability

Mankind's history is marked by a growing use of energy which until the end of the Industrial Revolution came largely from renewable sources. It was coal that fed the furnaces and boilers of the Industrial Revolution from the end of the seventeenth century to the nineteenth century, and drove railway transport and steamships. As well as being a useful source of mechanical energy, it was also used in the manufacture of coal gas for street lighting and in the chemical industry. In fact, coal was the principal form of energy until 1900.

Discoveries at the beginning of the nineteenth century allowed the use of electricity and revealed the relations and the interconvertibility of different forms of energy. The principles of conservation and of energy quality did not become operative until much later. Meanwhile, in 1882, the first system for producing and distributing electricity in a large city was installed. This was the beginning of the second phase in industrialization through electrification.

Following the first successful oil drillings in 1859, Standard Oil, the first of the modern large scale oil companies, attempted the first vertical structure for overall control of the oil process. It involved extraction from the subsoil, storage, refining and final distribution. Later, the growth of derivatives, the lower extraction costs compared to coal and the greater ease and economy of transport made oil modern society's basic energy source.

The internal combustion engine led to motorization on a massive scale by land, sea and air and guaranteed a constantly growing market for petrol. The forties marked the start of the new petrochemical industry, which gave rise to an enormous number of new products; synthetic rubber, plastic, medicines, cosmetics, varnishes, artificial fibres, detergents, weedkillers, fertilizers, butane, propane, etc., opening the way to the mass-production of consumer goods and introducing new, non-biodegradable substances into the environment.

After World War II, ambitious programmes to produce electricity from nuclear energy were begun, in the search for a return on the enormous amounts of money invested. The economic expansion in the West during the fifties and sixties was directly related to enormous petrol consumption at a time when energy was considered plentiful and cheap. Energy consumption during these decades grew more than exponentially. The fastest developing industrial sectors were precisely the ones that consumed most energy—petro-chemical industries, metallurgy, car manufacturing, domestic appliances, electricity generating, etc.—and a trend developed towards goods and services with higher energy intensity. Since 1950, increased energy production has been systematically favoured over more rational use. So much so that the increase in energy consumption has been taken as a reliable indicator of progress.

## The Aftermath of the Oil Boom

The oil crises of 1973 and 1980 showed up the fragility of an energy system that was over-dependent on oil. The War in the Gulf was reminder of what was at stake for the Western economies; free access to cheap oil in the Middle East. It was therefore fear of the hardship caused by the first crisis that brought about a change in attitudes in Western countries; efforts were directed at breaking free from this dependence, diversifying supply sources, perfecting replacement energies and promoting energy-saving programmes.

The eighties marked a change in people's awareness about environmental problems. The damage was making itself felt in more and more places and eventually the global threat to our planet as a result of our energy system became clear; the composition of the atmosphere was changing and could lead to possible changes in the climate.

According to recent figures, 82% of all the energy consumed in the world is produced by burning fossil fuels, 7.5% from burning biomass, 5.5% from the use of hydraulic energy and 5% from nuclear energy. Most of our energy in other words, in non-renewable; it runs out as we use it, as the population increases; and it comes from fossil fuels, which on burning increase the amount of $CO_2$ in the atmosphere. If we add to this the accumulation of nuclear waste, the problems of access to oil deposits, constant spillages during transport and all the different imbalances involved in the world energy system, the outlook is far from sustainable.

The inequalities speak for themselves; globally, less than a quarter of the world's richest population consumes almost three quarters of the energy commercialized in the world. For example, the average annual consumption per capita in the United States is 26 times higher than in India.

## The Choice of Change

Opening the way to societies that make sustainable use of energy necessarily involves increasing and improving energy efficiency, both in supply technologies and in end-use technologies, at the same time using renewable energy sources instead of fossil fuels.

Choosing the right system for the transformation of primary energy sources into energy services such as lighting, cooling, cooking, mechanical force, transport, etc. and choosing the most suitable appliances and technologies in each case is fundamental.

The truth is that a good standard of living is possible without wasting anything like as much energy. A series of relatively straightforward measures today allow a far higher level of comfort than in 1950, using one third as much energy for heating water for washing in the home.

Petrol consumption by vehicles has dropped by 40% in forty years, from 8 litres/100 kilometres to 5.3 litres in some models, and the work of improving their energy efficiency continues. In industry, the energy consumption necessary for manufacturing large intermediary products (steel, cement, paper or fertilizer) is decreasing steadily at a rate which varies between 0.5% and 0.2% per year according to the product.

Today's incandescent bulbs consume one twentieth as much electricity as bulbs in the twenties. The compact fluorescent bulbs now available can cut this down again to one fifth. Efficiency in lighting has increased one-hundredfold. The use of new materials and a more rational use of traditional materials allows a reduction in the amount of energy and raw materials consumed. Building a house, for example, requires 20% less energy than in 1950; building a vehicle, 40% less. On a global level, reducing our society's energy-intensiveness is the first step towards energy sustainability.

# 13

# Energy:

## *A Fair Deal for All*

Both the supply of energy and the demand for it have spiralled in modern societies, where everyday life and changes to the environment, global as well as local, are conditioned by energy production and use. There is a crying need for a fairer share-out of material goods, energy and economic resources.

Engery comes in three forms: So-called "fossil" fuels (coal, oil and natural gas); nuclear power; and "renewable" energies (hydroelectric power, thermal or photovoltaic solar energy, wind and tide power, wood, etc.). Each of these has its own undeniable advantages and drawbacks.

### Fossil Fuels

Fossil fuels are abundant and very simple to use. Oil, for example, can be very easily transported and processed, and is relatively cheap. The technology for producing its many derivatives is highly developed. What's more, it is particularly well suited for use in all forms of land, sea and air transport. Its handy fluid form and its price make it appropriate to the needs of poor communities or those that are unable to invest in capital goods.

Fossil fuels account at present for 77 per cent of all the energy produced and will, according to the most realistic projections, still account for 73 per cent in 2020. The resources will be strictly limited geographically as well as in duration, being restricted to certain regions. This state of affairs is fraught with the risk of tensions and even conflicts, owing to the strategic importance of energy supplies.

Fossil fuels, are furthermore, responsible for the manmade increase in the carbon dioxide content of the earth's atmosphere, with the associated danger of an increase in the greenhouse effect and, as a direct result, global warming of the order of 1° to 4°C in the next twenty years, which would adversely affect the climate and the environment. Though much uncertainty remains as to the scale of these effects, the risk is great enough to mean that every effort should be made to slow down the increasing "carbonization" of the atmosphere due to the intensive use of fossil fuels.

**Nuclear Power**

The main advantage of nuclear power is that it has no effect on the carbon dioxide content of the atmosphere. As it is also cheaper (per energy unit) than hydroelectric or thermal energy, some countries, have opted strongly for this way of producing electricity.

Nuclear power is, however, far from being unanimously accepted. Public opinion is very conscious of the lack of candid information and of the safety of nuclear plants, two aspects that have not always been treated, in some countries, with all the necessary care and clarity by the authorities and the operators. The public is also worried about the disposal of long-lasting radioactive wastes, an acute problem to which the experts seem confident that a long-term solution can be found. It would also be a mistake to underestimate the danger of the spread of nuclear arms, even though the main powers are now significantly reducing their arsenals of these weapons. A final point is that only those countries which can afford to make the huge investments required can put nuclear plants into operation. The investment is offset by the low cost of the fuel but is recouped only in the medium and long term.

**Renewable Energy Sources**

The ecological movements, which are worried both by global warming and by the real or imagined dangers of nuclear power, would like renewable energy sources to be developed faster than is now the case. These forms of energy at present supply some 18 per cent of total demand, which puts them well ahead of nuclear power.

Technology is moving repidly forward in this field. These forms of energy are capable of meeting the needs of communities that it would be too expensive to connect to a central grid supply, but despite improved productivity and falling costs, they remain on the whole dearer than the two previous forms. It will be a long time before they can constitute the main source of supply. Other problems that remain to be solved include the major investments required for hydroelectric power stations and the environmental damage caused by the building of dams and wind farms.

We must face the fact that as of now there is no "miracle" energy that is risk-free for humans and their emvironment and is also cheap and inexhaustible. There is no such thing as absolute security as regards power generation and use, and it will not be possible in the future to do without any of the above-mentioned sources. Energy demand will continue to grow as a result of irreversible technological advances, of the justified demands of the non-industrialized countries, and of population growth that is in any case set to continue for at least the next fifty years.

**Some Ethical Principles**

A number of imperatives must thus be borne in mind by every individual, every nation and, in particular, the citizens of the industrialized countries. These are: the right of each individual to sufficient sources of energy; our responsibility towards our children and our children's children, protection of the environment; prevention of the potential major risks from the production of energy on a massive scale; the control of costs and the need to carry on with research in all these fields.

Some of these obligations—those relating to population growth, climate change or the disposal of nuclear wastes, for example—are of a very long-term nature, while others—effort to deal with pollution caused by road transport or chemical waste disposal—are short-term. These differences of time-scale and the various possible interactions between the quantitative and qualitative aspects of the question have to be taken into account in observations of an ethical character such as the following:

- The present situation, wherby nearly one person in four in the world is without access to the energy resources he or she requires, cannot be accepted with resignation. Those with an active role in energy policy-decision-makers, industrialists, research workers and so forth—must ultimately ensure that there exist, and continue to exist, sufficient resources of sufficiently cheap energy for all countries to have acess to them, regardless of their geographical or economic situation.
- There should be no pretext for unnecssarily keeping the countries of the South, which urgently need proper infrastructures, on short commons as regards energy use. This is one area where, more than in any other, people need to be informed, so that they can take part in discussion and decision-making on subjects where scientific and technological knowledge is essential.
- Our duty to future generations enjoins us to use energy resources as sparingly and rationally as possible, especially as we know that a major part of these resources may be exhausted in a century or two.
- Even though rapid progress is being made in the exploration of space, we must acknowledge the obvious fact that we have only one Earth and must therefore preserve and protect it. Since energy production and use may jeopardize our environment, there is an urgent need for appropriate measures to be taken as rapidly and as effectively as possible. The management of nuclear waste and campaigns to combat all forms of pollution arising from energy use constitute unconditional obligations in this connection.
- Whenever massive quantities of nuclear or other forms of energy are produced or transported, e.g. when oil is transported by sea or big dams are built, major risks

to life and health ensure. Absolute safety is unattainable, but the various energy authorities are nevertheless under an obligation to issue and enforce appropriate safety regulations.

- Unit cost will continue to be the main factor influencing the choice between different forms of energy. Production costs must be controlled and savings constantly sought if energy supplies are to be available to all.
- Research sometimes seems to have been neglected in work on energy production and consumption, but it is an indispensable duty. Efforts to find new sources of energy and more economical ways of using it must continue.

**Further Recommendations**

We must keep our eyes open for the early warning signs of potentially dangerous or irreversible situations, and react quickly to them.

Application of the "precautionary principle" remains an unconditional obligation. We must take economic and fiscal measures designed to avert the risks of tension between producers and consumers and to encourage proper control of the resource in question. The tax instrument should be used to redistribute resources between privileged and less privileged groups of the population.

The man and woman in the street and their elected representatives must be informed about everything relating to the production and consumption of every kind of energy. Parliaments should have their own scientific and technological evaluation services, as is the case in certain countries. Projections made on the basis of different economic and demographic hypotheses ought to be regularly updated.

Now it is realized that no form of energy can replace any other form, we must endeavour to preserve the balance between producers and consumers, between rich and poor and between those that are spendthrift and those that are thrifty.

# 14

# Population Growth and Energy

It has been scarcely 200 years—the dawn of the Industrial Revolution—since humans abandoned sole reliance on firewood, other biomass fuels, and direct sunlight to meet daily energy needs. In the past half-century, global demand for energy grew twice as fast as population, as industrial nations burned coal, oil, and natural gas to fuel their economies. Over the next half-century, world energy demands are projected to continue expanding beyond population growth, as developing countries try to catch up with industrial nations.

Developing countries will see tremendous growth in energy consumption in the next half-century, as growing populations and increasing affluence combine to drive their energy demands to dizzying levels. Based on projections from the U.S. Department of Energy and the Intergovernmental Panel on climate change, total energy consumption in the developing world will grow by 336 per cent—nearly three times faster than population—over the next 50 years, from 3,499 million tons of oil equivalent to 15,255 million tons. By 2030, energy consumption in the developing world will likely surpass usage in industrial nations.

Rising per capita consumption accounts for nearly two thirds of the growth in energy demand in poorer nations, but different population trajectories can have dramatic effects on future demands. For example, assuming the same growth in per capita energy demand, moving to the low U.N. population projection will reduce total energy demands from developing countries by 2,792 million tons of oil equivalent—the output of nearly 3,000 average-sized coal-fired power plants.

In the next 50 years, the greatest growth in energy demands will come where economic activity is projected to be highest: In Asia, where consumption is expected to grow 361 per cent, though population will grow by just 50 percent. Energy consumption in Latin America and Africa is projected to increase by 340 per cent and 326 per cent, respectively. Lower rates of population growth in Asia, compared with Latin America and Africa, mean that energy use per person will increase most in Asia. Nonetheless, in all three regions, local pressures on energy sources, ranging from forests to fossil fuel reserves to waterways, will be significant.

When per capita energy consumption is high, even a low rate a population growth can have significant effect on total energy demand. In the United States, for example, where current per capita energy demand is nearly double that in other industrial nations and over 13 times that in developing countries, the 75 million people projected to be added in the next 50 years will boost energy demands by 758 million tons of oil equivalent—roughly the same as the present energy consumption of Africa and Latin America.

World energy use per person doubled between 1950 and 1973, before confronting a short-term slowdown when restricted exports from oil-producing nations drove up energy prices. Another price shock, combined with a global economic recession, resulted in the slowdown of the early 1980s. The most recent stumbling block in energy growth followed the 1989 revolution in Eastern Europe, when energy use in the former Soviet states plummeted. Although DOE and IPCC project substantial future growth, similar force may act to check such a development.

World oil production per person reached a high in 1979 and has since declined 23 per cent. Moreover, estimates of when global oil production will peak range from 2011 by petroconsultants to 2025 by the IPCC, signaling future price shock as long as oil remains the world's dominant fuel. Although people born in 1950 saw per capita oil production quickly double in a few short decades, those born in 2000 are likely to see it cut in half, dropping below 1950 levels.

In addition, meeting increased energy demands will require more storage an transportation infrastructure. Communities without a reliable supply of clean water or an adequate system for waste disposal may also fall short in connection to power supplies. For the estimated 2 billion who are still off the grid—and also experiencing high rates of population growth—decentralized energy technologies, such as solar roof shingles and fuel cell power generators, are likely the most feasible and affordable option for meeting increased energy demands.

Yet it will not necessarily the scarcity of fuel that constrains future growth in energy consumption, but rather concerns about climate change, air quality, and water quality. Growing climate concerns will require massive reductions in fossil fuel use at a time when demand for energy is soaring. A shift to renewable energy sources, such as solar energy and wind power, in addition to continued efficiency gains for power plants, cars, and appliances, holds great promise for meeting future energy demands without adverse ecological consequences.

# 15

# Not Yet Fossil Fuel

People were gathering wood for their fires more quickly than it could grow back. In India, wood was being burned 50 per cent faster than replacement tress were growing. Among environmentalists, the perception became widespread that village cooking fires were consuming the Indian forest.

Firewood demand was a minor cause of deforestation. People were mostly using twigs and dead braches for fuel, leaving trees standing. The main perpetrators of deforestation were not women preparing for the evening meal, but farmers clearing land for crops and livestock. To this day, however, the belief persists that fuel wood scarcity drives deforestation. That popular misconception has hampered efforts to address serious fuel wood problems that do exist. While not quite deforest ating the globe, these problems are undermining the well being of millions of people in India.

Until recently, most biomass consumer lived n rural areas. As populations have grown, and the number of trees has diminished, searching for fuel wood has indeed become a demanding task. In some areas of India for example, collecting firewood was a two-hour task only a generation ago, yet today it is almost an entire day's expedition—every day. That constitutes an enormous erosion of productivity in other kinds of work. And the problem is worsening rapidly.

What makes the situation even more difficult is that fuel wood problems have now spread from rural areas to the cities. In the 1950s, the cities in India were relatively small, inhabited mainly by those who could afford such "modern" fuels as kerosene, liquefied petroleum gas (LPG), and electricity. But in the past three decades, urban populations have exploded as migrants from the rural areas pour into the cities in search of jobs and higher standards of living.

Despite the availability of the "modern" energy sources to some of the city dwellers, the majority of migrants cannot afford them. Wood remains their fuel. But instead of collecting it, they now must buy it from vendors.

Biomass traders search for wood in communal woodlots, and consequently procure it as a "free" commodity. The price of the wood, which represents only the transport costs and traders' markups, excludes the production and replacement costs—at the expense of rural people and the natural resource base. After decades of woodland exploitation in some areas of India, the shortage of firewood in rural areas has become so severe that villagers are compelled to use cow dung, dried leaves, and grass for fuel. The fragile soils of the farmlands are thus denied essential nutrients and organic matter.

Villagers are working hard to reduce the exploitation of their resource base by the urban entrepreneurs. For example, in a village not far from, the capital city of Delhi, residents decided to charge traders for wood taken from their communal land. Extension agents were brought in to train the villagers in negotiating wood prices maintaining accounts, and establishing an agro forestry project. The revenue from wood sales is now used by the villagers to plant trees that will not only provide fuel for their personal use and for sale, but can be used for other purposes such as construction.

Dependence on wood for fuel is not just a challenge to economic sustainability, but a threat to Indians health. In the homes of low-income families, where traditional wood stoves are widely used for cooking, adequate ventilation is often lacking. The stoves require large quantities of wood, are unable to retain heat for prolonged periods, and send much of the fuel up in smoke. Inhaled by women an they cook, the smoke has been identified as a major cause of respiratory problems such as bronchitis, and of damaged eyesight.

Improved wood and charcoal stoves are now for sale in, India. Because they require significantly smaller quantities of firewood or charcoal, they are successfully curbing the wood demand, and hence promoting biomass conservation.

In the cities, as vendors travel longer distances into the hinterland in search of wood, and the transportation costs increase, more of the market is shifting to charcoal, which is easier to transport and more convenient to use in cramped urban quarters. However, widespread use of charcoal puts even greater stress on the environment because conversion from wood to charcoal requires twice as much timber to yield the same cooking energy.

In addition, once the conversion, transportation and combustion processes have been accounted for, charcoal emerges as one of the leading producers of carbon dioxide—the most prevalent greenhouse gas. A meal cooked with charcoal produces three times more carbon dioxide than the same meal cooked with wood. On the other hand, charcoal can be made into a more efficient fuel by producing it in kilns that retain a higher proportion of the energy content within the charcoal. And the amount of charcoal used can be reduced by the use of more efficient charcoal stoves, which control airflow to the fuel and are insulated to minimize heat loss.

Looking for alternatives to fuel wood and its charcoal derivative, a number of communities are experimenting with solar box cookers and biogas digesters, both of which use renewable sources of energy and are pollutant-free and energy efficient. The solar cooker and the digesters have been successful on a small and localized scale. The new methods have not been used on a big scale because of the high initial costs—along with a variety of cultural biases and superstitions. For example, preparing and cooking food is an evening social activity, and solar cookers have to be used during the day. Biogas digestors or is similarly constrained, since in some cultures the use of human and livestock waste, as fuel is unacceptable.

The fuel wood crisis is complicated one, and the easy, large-scale solutions that were originally recommended, such as the establishment of peri-urban plantations to increase wood fuel supplies, evidently will do little, if anything, to alleviate the problem. However, over the years, through mistakes and project failures, a few useful lessons have been learned. One such lesson—counter-intuitive though it may seem to many environmentalists—is that since biomas fuels will continue to play a major role for years to come, greater emphasis needs to be placed on finding ways to increase the wood fuel supply. Farmers, for example, can be encouraged to plant trees that will provide not only fuel but other products such as fruits, fodder, and lumber. And when the new high-efficiency stoves are made more widely available, the demand for trees will be reduced—even as their supply is increased.

# 16

## Turning on the Heat:

### *India's National Programme on Solar Cooking*

Anyone who has ever watched a pot of water being boiled just by the sun is sure to have been impressed. High-quality solar cooker can reach temperatures over 200ºC. This temperature is more than sufficient to cook food, bake bread and heat up an iron for ironing clothes. As rural people in many parts of the world heavily depend on wood for preparing meals, solar cooking can also make an important contribution to saving our forests. But even after three decades of implementation, solar cookers have not evolved into commercially viable products that sell themselves. India is the country with the most experience in this field.

The principle behind solar cooking is as fascinating as it is simple: sunrays are converted to heat and conducted into the cooking pot. Solar cooking also has some practical advantages: solar power is inexhaustible, clean and free. By lessening their dependency on conventional fuels people can save money and non-renewable resources as well as the environment. The solar cookers often make use of a box or parabolic reflector to concentrate the sun's rays.

In India some 4,75,000 solar cookers were sold last year with the help of government grants and highly subsidised prices. That puts India way ahead of all other countries. In rural homes—70 per cent of the Indian population lives in rural areas—cooking accounts for a major share of total energy consumption. The available energy sources are firewood, crop residues and animal dung: In urban and semi-urban areas, gas, kerosene oil and coal are used for cooking purposes. The smoke emitted from these fuels pollutes the environment and the kitchen, affecting the health of the family members, especially the women. Fuel wood is becoming scarce due to the depletion of forest.

**Solar Energy is Abundant**

Solar cooking has long been envisaged as a solution to mitigate these problems. After all, solar energy is abundantly available in most parts of the country. The daily average solar energy incidence ranges between five and seven kmwhr/m2 and there are as many as 250 to 300 clear sunny days a year. On such days it is possible to cook both mid-day and evening meals in a solar cooker. It is, however, recognised that solar cooking cannot fully replace conventional fuels. The government of India first initiated efforts in the early 1980s to popularise solar cooking devices all over the country in order to reduce dependency on conventional fuels.

**National Programme Launched**

A national programme on solar cooking was launched during 1981-82, which promoted above all the box-type cooker on account of its relative advantages. The concentrating types were not selected due to their high cost. The need for frequent tracking and the fast deterioration of reflecting surface etc. A subsidy of 33 per cent of the cost was granted by central government. In some states, an additional subsidy was also provided. To maintain the quality of the solar cookers being marketed, standard specification were developed and given to all manufactures and state agencies. Extensive efforts were also made to promote a wide network of manufacturers so that, over the years, around 55 manufacturers established units. The programme driven by the subsidy scheme was continued until 1994, when it was decided to adopt a market orientation and introduce new arrangements.

Studies to monitor practical benefits were conducted and revealed that while over 70 per cent of the owners were using their cookers, many did not use them frequently. The rest were not cooking with them at all due to climate problems, non-availability of open space, time constraints or cooker being out of order. Main requirement in the field of service were found to be the black-painting of tray and vessels, removal of moisture between glazings, replacements of broken glasses and prevention of hot air leakage. Shortcomings of the programme itself also became clear. As the manufacturers delivered the cookers to the state agencies who were selling them on they were mainly interested in supplying cookers and gave insufficient attention to after-sale service for the product. They were not interested in developing their own sales and services network. This meant that customers could not get a model of their choice. All these factors finally led to the termination of the subsidy regime.

**New Commercialisation Strategy**

In order to give the programme a stronger market orientation, a new strategy was evolved in 1994 aimed at the commercialisation of solar cookers. Under this scheme, manufacturers were allowed to make modifications to the cooker design to make them more attractive and user-friendly. Sales were allowed both through state agencies and directly by manufacturers through their own network.

Certain negative trends have also emerged: Contrary to the original intention, it has become apparent that most solar cookers were being sold in Cities and suburban areas. A price of 25 to 60 US dollars depending on the model—is still too high for the rural population. Nevertheless, the programme focuses on commercial success in view of the excellent progress now being made. Th market-oriented programme is leading to the creation of independent distribution networks, better customer service and user-friendly models. However, commercialisation has, for the time being at least, brought higher prices and falling output. "Low-cost but durable models still need to be developed for wider dissemination of the technology in rural areas.

**Sales Showrooms**

A new initiative by the government is focusing on the establishment of showrooms for the sale and servicing of renewable energy products (including solar cookers) in major cities of the country. With financial help from the government they will offer over-the-counter sales of different renewable energy products disseminate information and carry out repair and servicing of the equipment. These solar shops, which operate under the name of "Aditya" (meaning Sun in Sanskrit), allow manufactures from all over the country to present their solar cookers and other products to the public. The average sale during the last five years have numbered 25,000.

To boost the sale of solar cookers and provide after sale services to users, a new scheme for self-employed workers (SEWs) has been introduced in 1999. Under this scheme, state agencies enlist a set of SEWs in their respective states who will receive training in the repair of solar cookers and in their proper use and preparation for various types of cooking. These SEWs will be recruited among unemployed youths with a technical qualification and experience in mechanical work. The scheme worker is to act as a link between the users and the manufacturers and banks. The SEWs shall receive a nominal payment per cooker as a promotional incentive for selling more cookers in his area.

Never were these cookers more necessary than today. Wood burning still meets 15 to 18 per cent of primary energy consumption—more that nuclear any hydropower together. Greater demand for fuelwood is not only leading to desertification, it will also leave a growing number of people (the FAO puts the figure already at two billion) without enough energy toprepare themselves a regular hot meal.

# 17

## Between Wish and Reality:

### *The Limited Potential of the Solar Cookers*

Efforts to promote the idea of using solar cookers have been made for decades, but despite great commitment they have failed. Nowhere has it come to self-sustaining commercial dissemination of these cookers. Above all, it has not been possible to reach; the main target group, the rural population. But that has not detracted from the fascination of using the sun to cook.

**The Indian Experience**

Most experience with solar cookers has been gathered in India. The National Physical Laboratory in new Delhi tested the efficiency of cooking boxes and concentrating cooker back in 1953. Large batches were produced at the beginning of the 1960s, but evidently without lasting success. The meant when in 1981 a national programme to disseminate cooking boxes was launched it had to begin all over again. Over the course of time and with strong government promotion, 55 manufacturers began producing the units. Subsidies pushed the sales price down to half the production cost of US$ 60-70, and in low-income areas even down to US$ 15.

At the same time, the government ran a radio, television and newspaper advertising campaign to promote the cookers, and roped in prominent figures to endorse them. Other promotions featured cooking demonstrations in villages, and giving a solar cooker as a prize for couples that danced best at parties. About 1,20,000 cookers were sold in the way by 1990.

But that was only a deceptive success. Random checks found that after a while most households used their solar cookers only occasionally. About 30 per cent no longer used them at all for various reasons.

The results were especially poor in the villages. A survey of rural energy consumption in six Indian federal states in 1996 found that of 51,000 households only 70 possessed a solar cooker. At the same time, the survey also refuted the oft repeated prejudice that the people opposed innovations and rejected them even when they were useful. After all, 6,200 of the households surveyed had bought a pressure cooker because they cooked faster and used less fuel.

India is now making a fresh attempt to propagate solar cookers. According to the Ministry of Non-conventional Energy Sources, almost 500,000 highly subsidized cookers were sold in 1998. It is not clear how better results are to be achieved this time. The programme director is surprised that most of the cookers are sold in town rather than in rural areas, although based on earlier experience nothing else was to be excecpted.

## Socio-Cultural Factors

The causes of the only modest success of solar cooking equipment lie less in the technical sector than in the socio-cultural, socio-economic and psycho-social area. This profound-sounding formulation identifies what is basically a simple fact. Solar cookers function, but they cannot replace the customary cooker. Even in arid zones the sun does not always shine, and in the mornings and evenings cooking must anyway be done by customary methods. That means solar cookers are a supplementary way of cooking that saves fuel. Experience has shown, however, that it saves at most one-third of usual fuel consumption. That is not fundamental progress for a household, only a degree of improvement. It is quite different from the situation in, for example, the photovoltaic (PV) sector, which enables completely new things such as electric light and radio reception. So it is not surprising that small, portable PV systems are very much in demand even among Tibetan nomads.

By contrast, a solar cooker is rated by purely economic criteria. Savings of time or money are balanced against the cost of the unit and its limits. Not all meals can be cooked on a solar cooker, preparation takes longer, and the cooking process can no longer be controlled as one like because it is determined by the amount of energy the sun offers. These disadvantages are not due to any particular shortcomings of the solar cooker as such which could be remedied by further development, but to the vagaries of the sun itself as a source of energy.

## Tibet as a Special Case

The only region in the world where solar cookers are firmly established is Tibet. A total of 70,000 to 1,00.000 units are estimated to be in use among a population of two million. But Tibet is a special case in which several favourable conditions for hours of sunshine per year, or an average of eight hours per day, and the intensity of its solar radiation is so high that with only a few exceptions solar cooking is possible throughout the whole year. Since sunshine in Tibet means almost always direct radiation, concentrators with parabolic reflectors are used.

On the other hand, Tibet has an extreme shortage of other fuels. Firewood in simple not available. There are hardly any trees in the mountains. Other traditional sources of fuel such as shrub, yak dung or turf are also extremely scarce and hardly available for the inhabitants of the three cities of Lhasa, Shigatse and Gyantse. They are dependent on cylinder gas or kerosene that must be brought in over thousands of kilometers from China and is correspondingly expensive.

Local eating habits also favour the use of solar cookers. For the yak butter tea Tibetans drink incessantly throughout the day a household needs a continual supply of hot water. The concentrator cookers, which can boil five litres of water in 15-20 minutes, are highly suitable for that. They are also used to cook rice, but very little for other meals. The structure of Tibetan housing areas is another factor favouring solar cookers, their enclosed courtyards and flat roofs providing, plenty of space for setting them up. All that has resulted in almost every urban household possessing a solar cooker. But use of the cookers is rural areas in much less widespread because the people have less money and transporting the heavy units to villages is difficult and expensive.

## Regional Contribution

Favourable conditions like those in Tibet are seldom to be found anywhere else. Viewed realistically, solar cookers are not the global solutions to the firewood crisis. At best, they make a regional contribution. Portraying the dissemination of solar cookers as a benedictory concept also does not help it further. Most of the solar cooker enthusiasts are still far from this insight. The World Solar Cooking and Food·Processing Conference, held in Varese, Italy, last October and attended by 300 experts from 64 countries, once again provided abundant material in support of solar cookers. The conference's final statement said: "Solar cooking has the potential to be one of the most significant contributions to solving the firewood problem."

# 18

## Sustainable Cities

Today almost one half of the world's population lives in cities. The world's cities are growing by one million people each week. Cities today play a significant role in development. They continue to attract migrants from rural areas because they enable people to advance socially and economically. Cities offer significant economies of scale in the provision of jobs, housing and services, and are important centres of productivity and social development.

However, the stress of this rapid urban population growth is often overwhelming. The long list of afflictions includes urban poverty rates of up to 60 per cent. Despite growing investments, more than one third of the urban population live in substandard housing. Forty per cent of urban dwellers do not have access to safe drinking water or adequate sanitation. Primarily due to a rapid growth and a deteriorating urban environment, at least 600 million people in human settlements (cities, towns and villages) already live in health-and life-threatening situations, and almost 50 per cent of these are children.

The high rate of urban population growth in most regions has led to common problems: congestion, lack of funds to provide basic services, a shortage of adequate housing and declining infrastructure, to name a few.

While these problems are occurring in urban areas, cities still have an important role to play in protecting the global environment in the face of rapid urban population growth.

Agricultural and livestock production in rural areas are pushing farther and farther into ecologically fragile regions and cannot support growing population. The finite land and water resources make it imperative that human settlements be carefully planned. Indeed, sustainable urbanization will ease the pressures caused by encroachment on fragile natural habitats.

India's cities offer a bewildering sight to any visitor: the congestion caused by rapid population growth and a continuing rural-urban drift often leads to conditions which defy all rules of orders, hygiene and environmental safety. Inadequate leadership, corruption and mismanagement have a harmful effect on the physical, environmental, social and ethical structures of cities in India.

Millions of people live in inadequate conditions—without piped water, electricity, security of land tenure, access to roads or health facilities. The means available for production and financing of housing and urban infrastructure are too limited to meet basic needs.

## Reducing Poverty and Creating jobs

Urban poverty is rising at an alarming pace, especially among women. The informal economic sector—which makes a substantial contribution to the delivery of services, production of goods, building of infrastructure and housing construction—often provides the only opportunity for the urban poor to make a living.

Local informal housing construction, for example, generates up to 20 per cent more jobs than high-cost construction. Street hawking, waste recycling and food production are primary sources of income among the urban poor and are illustrative of the creativity of survival strategies.

However, the informal sector itself is often highly exploitative and fails to raise people's economic development beyond mere subsistence. Larger economic strategies and more participatory urban planning approaches that take stock of local skills, technologies and materials are required to generate new and better-paying job opportunities in cities and towns.

## Incorporating Environmental Concerns

In 1992 the Rio Conference on Environment and Development designed the Agenda 21 Programme of action to help save a planet endangered by environmental neglect and plagued by poverty and underdevelopment. Most of the goals agreed to in Rio can become reality only through local action in cities where environmental threats are increasing. Again, it is the urban poor who are particularly endangered by environmental degradation and pollution. The world's Agenda 21 will fail if the city's environmental agenda (population, inadequate sanitation, water supply and waste management) is not addressed. This is being recognized by local authorities all over the world.

Sustainable development in the twenty first century will to a large degree, depend upon how cities, towns and villages everywhere interact with the environment and utilize natural resources.

## Increasing Awareness of Gender Issues

Women and men use and experience cities differently, according to their roles, responsibilities and access to resources. For example, when basic services are lacking in a settlement, more often than not it is women who take on responsibilities such as water collection and refuse disposal. Women often have unequal access to resources such as property, credit, training and technology. All of these factors must be addressed urgently, as they make it harder for women to improve their living standards and those of their children.

## Disaster Mitigation Relief and Reconstruction

As cities become large and more densely populated, they become increasingly vulnerable to natural and man-made disasters such as earthquake, floods, industrial hazards, epidemics, civil strife and wars. Poor people are forced to live in the mot exposed, dangerous and cramped conditions; in flood-prone areas, on steep hillsides or near polluted streams and waste dumps. As a result, they are most likely to lose their homes or their lives when disasters occur. Better planning, access to affordable urban land, and improved construction methods can reduce the extent of catastrophes.

These successful and sustainable approaches to poverty eradication; managing the urban environment; providing access to land, shelter and finance; empowering women and men; and many other issues will have to be documented and disseminated widely.

# 19

## Living with Diversity

Fishers' nets and loggers' saws may directly impoverish local ecosystems, but most biological losses have root causes far away, in long-settled urban areas and farms where diversity is seldom a concer, but where steadily rising demand for food, water, wood and other resource—and the dispersal of resulting wastes-reach far beyond the settled areas themselves. In general, these peopled landscapes have lost much of their own biological wealth, but what remains is still important to their continued functioning and livability. Reconciling farms and cities with diversity will require stopping the damage they bring to remaining natural habitats, but also beginning to halt and reverse the homogenization of these unnatural habitats.

Uniformity is not inherently undesirable. In fact, to some degree, homogeneity is the basis of all agriculture: a given type of plant is favoured and others are suppressed or eliminated. But trends in recent decades (most notably the Green Revolution and the parallel intensification of farming systems in industrial nations) have pushed uniformity to dangerous levels.

The unsustainability of modern agriculture is in part a measure of its inability to tolerate diversity. Both genetic and ecological uniformity—the sameness of fields sown horizon to horizon without interruption—demand costly and often futile reliance on chemicals to protect crops from pests or diseases that are rapidly spreading and evolving. The drive to leave no hectare unplowed worsens soil erosion, pushing tractors onto highly erodible hillsides and removing windbreaks, hedgerows and other remnant habitats.

Some of agriculture's biological impacts are obvious—the expansion of farms onto forests and wetlands, for example. While the increasing reliance on chemical inputs and machinery has reduced these impacts in some cases by decreasing the area needed to produce a given amount of food, it has worsened others.

A fundamental away transition from today's wasteful and polluting farming systems is needed to put the world's food supplies on a secure footing. Many of the reforms that will reduce farming's dependence on fossil fuel inputs and its misuse of soils and waters can also restore diversity to agricultural landscapes. Pesticides, for example, kill not only pests but other animals, such as pollinators and predators, that are beneficial to agriculture. Alternative pest control measures that lower pesticide use can also, ironically, reduce pest damage to crops by reviving the diversity of soil and insect communities, which play crucial roles in maintaining soil productivity and checking the spread of pest outbreaks.

Traditional agroecosystems are important not only because they provide sustenance to rural people and harbour valuable genetic resources, but also because they contain the seeds of a sustainable, diversity-based mode of agriculture. At varying levels, diversity is the basis of production for many peasants. Farmers often mix strains of a given crop in their fields as a hedge against the vagaries of weather. They also tend to recognize the dependence of their farms on adjacent ecological systems and to tolerate wild plants (often crop relatives whose continued interbreeding with domestic descendants contributes to genetic variety) on the outskirts of their fields.

Population growth and the expansion of large commercial farms have rendered many once-sound practices no longer viable, and traditional agriculture badly needs infusions of money and research to increase its modest yields without abandoning its stability.

Urban areas, with good reason, are considered the antithesis of natural diversity. Only the most resilient creatures (many of them regarded as weeds and pests) thrive in them, and cities' ceaseless expansion, consumption of resources and emissions of waste threaten both farmland and wilderness almost everywhere. As with agricultural lands, the first priority for urban areas is to half their expansion onto other ecosystems and reduce the damage they export, such as the sewage poured onto coral reefs by burgeoning coastal cities throughout the tropics, or the wasteful consumption of tropical hardwoods in Japanese building construction.

But even concrete jungles can support some diversity. Landscaping of private yards and public spaces with native vegetation can not only reduce the expense and environmental impact of watering, spraying and hauling the remains of sterile grass monocultures, but also help revive bird and other wildlife populations. Most urban areas also have water-ways running through them, or corridors of unused land such as steep ravines; if their use as waste receptacles is reduced, these can be maintained or restored as wildlife habitat.

In developing nations, especially, a surprising amount of agricultural production takes place within city limits, in home gardens. These hidden farmlands contain a great deal of genetic diversity, and their expansion could help reduce the scale and environmental impacts of commercial agriculture.

One reason that the destruction of biological diversity has gone so far without major public commitments to stopping it is that urban dwellers have little experience of the natural and even less understanding of its importance. Restoring nature where people live-reestablishing a personal link with the living world—may be necessary to save it elsewhere. For all the rational arguments favouring long-term protection of biological assets, people who have lost all direct sense of their dependence on natural systems may simply not care.

Only a growing respect for diversity for its own sake—beginning, perhaps, with a reconnection between people and nature within the urban environment—will trigger altruistic responses among those wealthy enough to have the option of considering the needs of future generations and natural communities. Although many conservation measures make economic sense, arguments of economics or self-interest will likely fail to be convincing when the contest is between a few uncharismatic species of unknown value and a major industrial project. "Human beings make sacrifices for what they love." Those who maintain strong bonds with the biological world on which they depend may be more inclined to make the hard decisions needed to protect it.

# 20

## Link Between Disability and Poverty

Disability affects nearly every fifth household in developing countries and is a prevalent contributing factor to family poverty.

An already poor household has an added financial burden when a disabled family member is not involved in productive activities. In the context of extreme poverty, a disability may sometimes turn into an asset when the person uses begging as a way to bolster the family income. But this is a degrading path that does not lead out of poverty.

What aggravates the situation is the fact that poverty is identified as one of the main causes of disability. This is especially so for those at the lowest strata of society who live in precarious conditions without education, hygiene and health care.

An important element of measures aimed at families living in absolute poverty is that they learn how to prevent disability. They must also learn that a disabled family member can take part in economic activities.

Increasing the economic usefulness of a disabled household member can help to reduce the poverty of many families. The income earned by the disabled person not only benefits him or her but the entire household as well.

However, anti-poverty strategies which target disabled household members without attempting to alleviate general household poverty would likely be futile.

One widespread misconception is that disabled people are unable to earn a living and to be self-reliant. As a consequence, disabled people are often targeted only for passive measure of income replacement and social welfare schemes. Active measure in their favour are conceived of as social activities and not economically relevant. Such misconceptions generate and reinforce exclusion, which in turn perpetuates poverty.

This highlights a dimension of poverty often overlooked by economists. They defined poverty only in terms of household income. But poverty also means to lack social status and to lose human dignity.

Thus a basic criterion for an anti-poverty strategy at the micro-level is whether it serves to establish human dignity. An approach, which merely dishes out state subsided or international aid to the destitute keeps the recipients in a position of dependence.

Targeting specific groups for poverty alleviation measures is always a highly sensitive issue. It can damage the fragile social fabric and may result in greater poverty for some while favouring others. Such a risk may be avoided through a participatory approach, which actively involves the poor and assists them in their efforts to gain control over their lives.

Disabled people are more likely to be poorer than their non-disabled peers because of the discrimination, which accompanies disability, not because of the impairment itself.

They suffer from social exclusion and frequently find themselves trapped in a web of neglect. The problem is even more acute for disabled women, who encounter enormous prejudices and obstacles in their quest to participate in social and economic life.

A more enlightened society will seek to integrate disabled people, to give them opportunities to learn and to wok as others do. It will adjust the physical environment to accommodate their special needs.

This planet belongs to all people. If some people are trapped somewhere, we must all come forward to remove the causes of their discomfort. At the same time we must leave our shores open for anybody who decides to join us, or anybody who decides to part our company.

Poverty denies a person control over his destiny. Poverty means not being able to tell what tommorrow would be like. If we examine the situation carefully we will see that the poverty is neither created by the poor, nor sustained by the poor. It is the system of policies and institutions that we have built around us that creates and sustains poverty. Poverty is the denial of human rights. Over one billion people live below the absolute poverty line right now on this planet are denied of almost all human rights. There is no way one can defend the existence of poverty anywhere. Poverty is a disgrace for the entire man-kind, Because we allow another humanbeing to die of hunger, or malnutrition, or common curable diseases, or exposure to climate, we are reduced to less humanbeings. If a particular would system is responsible for creating this massive poverty we must act to replace it.

Resource-wise or technology-wise, there is no reason why poverty should exist and continue to deepen and widen. If we make up our minds to wipe out poverty from the surface of the earth, the worst aspect of poverty can be removed within the next couple of decades.

Each humanbeing is a wonderful creation of the creator. Each humabeing is born with great potentials. Poverty denies any opportunity for a person to achieve any of his/her potential. We have built a world system which is in the habit of pushing people down not building them up. It creates barriers around individuals, rather than remove them.

The most effective step that we must take to remove poverty is to create a system which creates enabling conditions for people and removes the existing barriers. The institutional barriers were skillfully crafted over the centuries to benefit a handful of people.

Resource-poor nations with high incidence of poverty waste away enormous human capability each day by denying poor people the use of their energy and ingenuity. If they could have been made economically active, not only they could have contributed in the national production, they would have helped expand the domestic market for the products produced. The disabled one can be transformed into the engine of grwoth if we only allow them to unleash their capacity.

We cannot be at peace with ourselves if we know there is a humanbeing who lives a life worse than an animal. A humanbeing is supposed to live differently than an animal. He/she is supposed to live a life with human dignity. Human dignity is what distinguishes a humanbeing from an animal. When we cannot ensure this dignity for other's, our own dignity becomes an empty pretens.

There must be a thousand and one ways to remove poverty from the earth. We may or may not know some of those ways already. Obviously there are many more ways yet to be designed, each more effectively than others. When we shall find them, how many of them we shall find, how quickly we find them will depend on how eager we are to find them. But to say that poverty cannot be overcome, directly and quickly, is to underestimate the capacity of human mind.

# 21

# Food Production

During the last 25 year, world agriculture successfully expanded food production faster than population growth. This can continue for the next 25 years and beyond, if appropriate action is taken. Although world food stocks are currently low and grain prices high, the world is not about to run out of food. We can produce enough food for future generation if we choose to do so.

The widespread food insecurity, unhealthy living conditions, and abject and absolute poverty in many developing countries are already threatening global stability. Failure to assure sustainable food security will foster the very conditions that will further destabilize and polarize the world in the years to come with tremendous consequences for all people.

### The Basic Facts

Poverty is widespread in developing countries, with over 1.1 billion people living on a dollar a day or less per person. Human resource development in developing countries is lagging: 1 billion people lack access to health services, 1.3 billion do not have access to adequate sanitation systems, and one-third of primary school enrolls drop out by Grade 4. Natural resources, upon which future food production depends, are being degraded at alarming rates: almost 2 billion hectares of land have been degraded in the past 50 years: about 180 million hectares of forests have been converted to other uses during the 1980s, marine fisheries are collapsing around the world, and regional and seasonal water shortage afflict many developing countries.

Improved appropriate technology is essential to increase productivity. Yet low-income food deficit developing countries are grossly under investing in agricultural research and many are reducing their support.

It calls for sustained action six priority areas. First, we must selectively strengthen the capacity of developing country government to perform appropriate functions such as establishing or clarifying property rights, promoting private-sector competition in agricultural markets, and maintaining appropriate macro economic environments. Predictability, transparency and continuity in policy making and enforcement must be pursued.

## Investing in People

Second, we must invest more in poor people in order to enhance their productivity, health, and nutrition. It is not only unethical but economically wasteful that a large share of the World's population is malnourished, illiterate, sick, and without access to productive resources. Access to primary education, primary health care, reproductive care and family planning information, and clean water and sanitation must be assured for all people. Access by the poor to productive resources and remunerative employment must be improved. Empowerment of women must be supported.

Third, we must accelerate agricultural productivity. Agriculture is the lifeblood of the economy in low-income developing countries. In those countries, it provides up to three-quarters of all employment and half of all incomes. There are very strong links between agricultural productivity increases and broad-based economic growth in the rest of the economy. Agriculture is an engine of growth in low-income developing countries. National and international agricultural research systems must be mobilised to develop improved technologies focused on developing countries, and extension systems must be strengthened to disseminate the improved technologies and techniques. Low-income countries currently spend less than 0.5 percent of the value of agricultural production on agricultural research compared to 2 per cent spent on agricultural research in middle and high-income countries. An increase of agricultural research expenditures in low-income countries to at least 1 per cent of the value of agricultural output is urgently needed, with a longer term target of 2 per cent. National agricultural research must be supported by a vibrant international agricultural research system that undertakes research with large international benefits applicable across boundaries. Current investments in international agricultural research are grossly inadequate to provide the support needed by developing countries. It is of critical importance that agricultural research result in reduced unit costs of production. Such cost reductions will make food economically accessible to low-income consumers, and permit producer incomes to increase. To assure relevance of research and appropriate distribution of responsibilities, interactions between public sector agricultural research systems, farmers, private enterprises, and NGOs must be strengthened.

Fourth, we must assure sustainability in agricultural production and sound management of natural resources. Farmers, local communities, and governments must be encouraged to establish and enforce systems of rights to use and manage natural resources, to improve the way water is allocated and used, to reverse land degradation where it has occurred, to reduce the use of chemical pesticides and promote integrated pest management programmes, and to implement integrated soil fertility programmes in areas with low soil fertility. Local control over natural resources must be strengthened and local capacity for organisation and management improved. Investments in less-favoured geographical areas, that is, areas with agricultural potential, irregular rainfall patterns, and fragile soils must be expanded. Most poor people in developing countries reside in rural areas, and most rural poor reside in less-favoured areas. Yet, most investments, including agricultural research investments, still focus on the more-favoured areas. If we are serious about reducing poverty and protecting the natural resource base, the balance between the less-favoured and more-favoured areas must be redressed.

Fifth, we must reduce food-marketing costs in low-income developing countries. The cost of bringing food from the producer to the consumer is very high in many of these countries. Efficient, effective, and low-cost agricultural markets must be developed in order to bring these costs down. Inefficient state-run firms in agricultural in-put markets must be phased out; investment in developing and maintaining infrastructure, especially in rural areas, must be forthcoming; policies and institutions that favour large-scale, capital-intensive market agents over small-scale, labour-intensive ones must be removed; development of small-scale credit and savings institutions must be facilitated, and technical assistance to create or strengthen small-scale, labour-intensive competitive rural enterprises must be provided.

Sixth, we must expand and realign international development assistance. Many years ago, industrialised countries had agreed to allocate at least 0.7 per cent of the gross national product (GNP) to international assistance. Most countries have not reached or do not maintain this target. Not only must the industrialised countries increase international development assistance to reach the 0.7 per cent target, but they must realign it to low-income developing countries. Also contrary to the middle-and higher-income developing countries, the poorest countries are not able to gain access to capital from the rapidly expanding international commercial capital market. Developing countries in turn must seek measures to diversify sources of external funding, stem capital flight; and improve the effectiveness of the aid they receive.

# 22

## Food for the Billions

Will there be enough food to feed 8 billion people who will live on earth in 25 years' time? Surprisingly few people, at least in the industrial countries, seems to be overly concerned with this question. Whereas the world conferences on the environment, on women, human rights or social issues which were held in recent years were preceded and accompanied by intensive public debate, food does not seem to be a burning issue. Don't we have mountains of surplus food, people ask. Do we not have to pay our farmers to leave their land idle in order not to add to the glut on the world markets? And hasn't the Green Revolution ended famine even in countries like India which used to be a synonym for hungry people? So where is the problem?

The advance made in agricultural production since beginning against a background of imminent crisis are indeed remarkable. In only 20 years, yields of major crops like rice, maize and wheat in developing countries went up by 80 per cent, outpacing even the rapid increase in population. But this growth in yields has slowed down in recent years, and the aim of "food for all" is once again becoming elusive. About 800 million people still do not have access to enough food to meet their basic daily needs, nearly 200 million children suffer from protein and energy deficiencies, 88 countries—44 of them in Africa—have a deficit in food production.

Everyone wants to increase food security. The definition is that "food be available at all times, that all persons have means of access to it, that it be nutritionally adequate in terms of quantity, quality and variety, and that it be acceptable within the given culture". To achieve this goal, more food must be produced-much more, because we must not only adequately feed the 5.8 billion people already on earth, but also the additional two billion who will be added to world population in the next 25 years. Critics argue that the problem is not one of production alone, but one of poverty elimination. People are not hungry because there is no food, but because they have no money to buy it, these critics say. Available resources must be better distributed to end hunger in the world.

However, even if we succeed to eliminate poverty in the next few decades—a feat which appears highly unlikely—there would still be the need to boost production, because with rising incomes people also want to eat more and better food including meat. As can already be observed in the countries of East Asia, the newly acquired wealth leads to higher consumption levels which puts additional strains on available resources are getting scarcer. Agricultural lands are being degraded at alarming speed by erosion, salinity, desertification or disappear altogether due to urban or infrastructure development. It has been estimated that 40 per cent of productive land now has diminished capacity to supply benefits to humanity due to direct human impacts of land use. Water for agricultural purposes is getting scarcer almost everywhere, and there are hardly any land reserves to be brought into production to widen the agricultural base.

In this situation, there is no alternative to increasing and improving production from the existing land area. This can only be done through research which finds the best varieties which will bring the highest yields at the lowest cost to the environment. Sustainable agriculture is the key notion one that maintains bio-diversity, uses as little chemical inputs as possible and does not over-exploit water and soil resources.

In recent years, agricultural research has been neglected—partly because of the erroneous belief that with mountains of meat and lakes of milk further production increases were not desirable. Since global grain production has stagnated and world stocks have reached an alarmingly low level last year, there has been a noticeable change of mind. To raise the awareness among governments around the world that promotion of agriculture is urgent if hunger is to be avoided in the next century.

Important work is already being done by the international agricultural research institutes which promoted the Green Revolution in the sixties and seventies and are now again in the forefront of finding solutions to the daunting task of feeding 8 billion people by the year 2020. The International Rice Research Institute (IRRI) in the Philippines, the Maize and Wheat Research Institute (CIMMYT) in Mexico or institutes like ICARDA in Syria and ICRISAT in India which work on agriculture in semi-arid and dry areas, are all seeking solutions to the problem of raising production while at the same time preserving the environment. These institutions as well as national agricultural research institutions need all the support from the public and, of course, appropriate funding, to help them accomplish their task.

The scientists are optimistic that they can develop the varieties and farming systems which will allow mankind to feed everyone on earth well into the next century. But the task is not for the scientists alone. An economic and political order must also be in place which makes it possible to eradicate poverty and allow everyone to enjoy the benefits that science can offer. Feeding the billions is, therefore not only a scientific, but first and foremost a political.

# 23

## Aid Effectiveness as A Multi-level Process

Parallel to the widespread decrease of aid resources provided by donor countries to developing countries in recent years, debate and research on how to make aid more effective has become a major concern. Usually, it is suggested that decades of development assistance have at best produced marginal results in terms of improving development levels in the South. Little mention is made of donor's policy shortcomings and the negative impact of these on efforts aimed at reforming and redefining development cooperation in order to enhance aid effectiveness. The policy parameters and operating frameworks of existing aid and policies continue to inhibit higher degrees of aid effectiveness. In many donor countries, opinion polls indicate waning public support for development aid.

Increasingly, the moral case for aid is called into question and deeper world market integration tends to be seen as the panacea to continued economic decline and social destabilization in the South. Against this background, cooperation between donor and recipient actors is faced with a duel uphill struggle. First, fewer resources can be mobilized to meet growing developmental needs. On the other hand, to organise and manage development policies and programmes in a result oriented manner, grows more difficult. The threat of further aid cuts and of further drops of public support for providing aid become ever more real. A closer look at the organizational complexities and political constraints under which development cooperation is expected to perform effectively may help to improve current aid management approaches.

## Towards Conceptual Clarity

At first sight, catchy definitions of what constitutes effective aid might appear attractive to use, in particular with regard to economic indicators. The term "aid effectiveness" is easily used in the same vein as "efficiency", "significance" or "impact" of aid. At times, obsession to measure and demonstrate the results of aid supported development processes can be observed among policy-makers and administrators on the donor side. Still the understanding of aid and its effectiveness as being part and parcel of a cooperation relationship between donor and recipient side parties, is scarcely embedded in practice. To determine how to make aid more effective requires more than a quick impact analysis of an individual and perhaps even isolated development project. Consequently, defining the concept of aid effectiveness needs to take into account at what levels cooperation is focused on. To strive for sustainable and effective modes of development cooperation will entail the need to combine recipient ownership of the development process with donor accountability concerns.

Performance expectations cannot be exclusively placed on the recipient while donor interests, their aid management systems and procedures remain unchanged.

An extended and more analytical, process oriented definition should take into account four main aspects of aid effectiveness:

*(a)* Effective aid must relate to the building and/or strengthening of in-country aid management capacity;

*(b)* To maximize the degree of aid effectiveness, local ownership of the aid process is essential: from setting of priorities through policy formulation and implementation on to the evaluation stages of the process;

*(c)* Increasing recipient side capabilities to take charge of aid relationship, will need to be combined with arrangements to meet legitimate donor accountability concerns;

*(d)* Aid effectiveness is a two-faceted objective: its realisation is equally dependent on increased

transparency of donor motives and on dropping of nondevelopmental, political and economic aid objective of donors.

In addition a broader range of stakeholders in the aid relationship needs to be actively involved: extending beyond accountably government and implementing agencies, to include democratic institutions and organisations of civil society and of the private sector.

Applying any definition of aid effectiveness without disaggregating macro-economic data and taking into account country specificity will only lead to unhelpful generalisations about aid and its effectiveness. It would seem more appropriate to adopt working definitions against which to assess effectiveness of aid resources at a country-specific level. On such a basis one could expect to arrive at more reliable indicators of how well aid resources contribute to improving developmental standards and meeting existing needs.

### From Definition to Success—Key Requirements

Having reached agreement between the recipient and donor on what should constitute effectiveness of aid is only a starting point. Embarking on democratic, peaceful and participatory patterns of economic and social development must follow: to arrive at significant and lasting improvement in many of the least developed countries will be a long-term process. This being said, it is crucial to design and implement such forms of development cooperation which involve a wide range of recipient side actors, not only from the government side but also from civil society at large. Seen as a process of increasing inclusion of intended beneficiaries of aid, the commitment to decentralize as well as entrust aid and its management grows in importance.

To fully capture Third World development realities, policy frameworks inspired by neoliberalist-type of development concepts and theories are grossly inadequate. The views and positions on aid articulated in the World Bank and the IMF, or in many if not most bilateral aid administrations in OECD countries, represent only one side of today's international cooperation, namely the donor side. The major weakness to point out with respect to this locus of debate, is a profound under representation if not even a total absence of recipient experiences and perceptions on aid in general and on its effectiveness in particular. There should be little doubt that ignoring to not actively identifying and involving such perceptions, leads to strongly donor driven aid.

To circumvent recipient side insights and views on strengths and weaknesses of aid strategies and mechanisms, will result in limited local commitment and sense of ownership over the aid process. Mutual decision-making between donors and recipients remains a rare policy approach. Aid procedures that are based on local management and less control-oriented donor roles in the aid process are still exceptions in development cooperation.

Structurally, in terms of the policy environment within which development aid is expected to function, the overriding policy framework is general based on structural adjustment policies (SAP). But the underlying conclusion made by proponents of SAPs that these policies induce aid effectiveness, has yet to be proven valid. It must suffice at this point to emphasize that there is not a priori relationship between world market integration under structural adjustment and sustainable development in poor countries. Aid to these countries which is solely intended to reinforce fundamentally uneven and unequal patterns of world market integration should at be scrutinized critically.

Some central issues need to be addressed in the course of improving aid and its effectiveness:

- institutional dimensions of aid relationships require strong policy-attention, both on the donor and the recipient side;
- capacities to effectively identify and formulate aid priorities need to be strengthened in recipient countries;
- local capacities to sustain reform efforts must be reinforced.

## Levels of Intervention

If the design of aid and the terms upon which it is provided to a developing country are largely determined by the donor, the aid relationship can be characterised as essentially hierarchical. Recipient side views will rarely surface, as they are either not identified, or not well formulated. Possibilities of a recipient-led development strategies can be limited. Unless scope is provided to the recipient side actors to assume responsibilities, aid effectiveness is likely to remain low or fluctuating, and the sustainability of donor aid efforts will remain doubtful.

National planning processes and courses of national development in recipient countries should be seen as most effective where they are led under local responsibility and control. To arrive at this ideal situation, gaps need to be reduced and closed at the various intervention levels.

Donor aid resources provide valuable support for this process. Their effectivenss in meeting long-term objective of aid will need to be assessed on the basis of how well they perform at the different levels. Individual donors will expectedly perform differently at the various levels. What will prove to be the ultimate test for effectiveness is how well the donor aid performance accomplishes the broader objectives of development cooperation and how well it includes sustainable results.

In the analytical frameworks outlined here, development cooperation would seem to be confronted with the effectiveness gaps at the:

- structural level: International trade and investment patterns, debt problems and world market integration process appear as long-term constraining factors upon aid and its effectiveness;
- at the policy level, dialogue and partnership in development cooperation are instrumental factors in recluding planning and co-ordination gaps with regard to policy analysis and formulation;
- The institutional level is where pertinent capacity gaps exist: capacity development efforts of donors and

technical assistance measures play an important role in addressing weaknesses in aid effectiveness within a country's institutional setting;

- finally, at the level of aid projects (programmes), it is generally the lack of sustainability of aid interventions which causes development activities to falter once donor support decreases or stops. In addition to technical cooperation, financial and material inputs serve to maintain project momentum and goal realization: the issue of how to develop local capacity sufficiently in order for indigenous organisations to continue project activities initially supported by donor aid, remains the most important issue to address at this level.

## Fostering Aid Effectiveness

Donor and recipient development efforts are too of ten isolated from one another, or poorly coordianted. They fail to address managerial and implementation bottlenecks. Cross-sectorial linkages, as well as interdisciplinary approaches to aid problems are only slowly gaining ground. It is increasingly obvious, that decisions on aid issues are subjected to concerns outside of the responsible ministry: finance ministers, and unfortunately even defence ministers have a strong say in how much aid is to be provided, where it is to be concenrated and under what terms to be utilised. Inside of recipient countries, large portions of national budgets are allocated to non-development priorities with little or no impact on alleviating urgent poverty problems.

Development cooperation may make the biggest impact and be executed most effectively where donors and recipients agree upon multi-level aid strategies. To give an example: building a road to a remote rural area may well be done in an effective project manner: it is equally important to have a functioning transport authority in place to ensure maintenance of the roads. If this authority operates within a nationally defined infrastructure policy, best in accord with national trade and investment priorities, then the effectiveness of the project-level road building programme has a good chance of being high.

Institutional changes to set the stage for a profound reform process in development cooperation are needed. Reprioritising national budgets to reflect identified in country development needs may be one step. Setting up policy evaluation and formulation units can be complimentary measures. Deregulating markets and investment rules may serve to please donors, but dumping of cheap products which strangle local production efforts may easily result. Regional cooperation, including intensified South-South cooperation can provide some counterbalance. There are only a few areas where changes in the current system of development cooperation can occur, with a view to better manage the complexities of aid and the social, cultural, economic and political backgrounds against which they take place. The will and commitment to take policy action in both donor and recipient countries, through the broadest range of stakeholders and institutions as possible, will be the test for genuine efforts at improving development relations between North and South and organising cooperation effectively.

# 24

# Urbanization and the Environment

Is abandoning the cities the answer to the growing ecological problems of urbanization? The trend at any rate is in the opposite direction. At the beginning of this century, only every 10th person worldwide was a city dweller. At its end, more than half the global population will be urbanites. And most of the urban population growth will take place in the developing countries, led by Asia.

Compared to other parts of the world, however, the urbanization process in Asia is currently not even particularly far out in front. Worldwide, city dwellers account for 43 per cent of the total population. Industrial nations have an average urbanization rate of 72 per cent. Less industrialized countries have 34 per cent. In the Asia-Pacific region the rate is 30 per cent, in Latin America 72 per cent, and in Africa 33 per cent. The urbanization growth rate in a number of Asian countries has in fact slowed compared with earlier years. Nevertheless, not only industrialization, but also the increasing degree of urbanization has emerged as a growing burden on the environment in many Asian countries.

## Changed Urbanization Pattern in India

Environment burdens are just as much a problem in the old industrial nations as they are in India. But each group has a specific pattern of development. The urbanization process in India has proven to be more pollution-intensive than that in the old industrial nations of Europe and North America. There are several reasons for that:

- industrialization in India is restricted to a few locations which are often concentrated in and around capital cities. Although environmental damage continues to be minor at a national level, these locations have higher pollution levels than those ever reached in Industrial nations;
- furthermore, besides the strong regionalization of industries, the industrialization pattern of India shows a great diversity of environmental hazards. The trend to establish "last industries first", which is promoted by progressive industrialization, leads to a country producing certain dangerous materials before they have been covered by state regulations;
- the time factor has to be seen as an important element in the emergence of these already highly regionalized environmental burdens. In India industrialization and its concomitant urbanization is taking place within a ban population grew tremendously.

**Growing Environmental Damage**

Water pollution in India is caused mainly by domestic sewage. For example, households are responsible for 75 per cent of the pollution of the rivers. The domestic sewage problem got more and more out of control with growing urban populations. Pipe-based waste water systems are rare in this country. In India dealing with waste has an extremely low priority. The type of waste disposal depends mostly on what the cities can afford. The present level of air pollution is also very high.

**Innovative Approaches to Solutions**

Environmental protection and economic development are seen as contradictions. Economic development can only be achieved at the cost of higher levels of environmental pollution. And in reverse, if pollution is to be controlled and reduced this can only be done to the disadvantage of further development. In the meantime, however, numerous instances of successful urban environmental management are developing. They could help to change and subsequently break through the existing pattern of thinking. Thc following approaches can be viewed as important.

Combining regulations with incentives: The introduction of lead-free petrol and the mandatory equipping of new cars with catalytic converters is still by no means common in India. As numerous cars without catalytic converters are still able to use lead-free. Converters were then at first made compulsory for higher-powered cars, and later also for compact models.

Combining regulations with simple controls: Apart from general limitation of the number of cars in the city, its most important single measure to prevent traffic jams and the additional petrol consumption and pollutant emissions caused by them.

High economic growth in India has in fact led to a general reduction of poverty. But the distribution of income, particularly between urban and rural areas, has remained relatively constant. Urban environmental and traffic problems have increased heavily during the same period. These developments can be attributed to a certain pattern of official action (or "non action"):

- governments have made efforts in supplying roads, but neglected the demand for mobility.
- governments are preoccupied with supplying water, and have neglected follow up problems, above all the questions of waste water disposal and treatment. In Indian cities, for example, this leads to the absurd situation that due to the mushroom like growth of the cities and the increased water pollution linked with it, water must be brought in over ever greater distances and at ever greater expense;
- governments take a one-sided look at noxious substances. Concentrations of harmful substances in water and in the air are in fact checked, and some measures are taken against individual pollutants of single sectors (e.g. lead emissions by the transport sector).

But an integrated policy which operates integrated environmental management with the aim of comprehensively relieving the burdens on the environment has not yet been developed anywhere. To consider such a concept, it is necessary to cut loose from the customary way of approaching problems. It makes sense not to separate the problem areas from each other according to sectors and pollutants, but rather on the basis of their ecological impact.

Orienting on demand hits the core of the concept pg ecological modernization, which is about reducing the intensity of resource use (note, at this stage this does not yet mean the absolute reduction of inputs). At the same time, sights are set on a lower use of land with the same size of population, or also lower energy consumption with the same degree of added value or the same per capita income.

Finally, the importance of governments for creating framework conditions must be emphasised once again. Because the actors come from different spheres, such conditions are essential.

From the time of the Greek polis, it was the ambition of the Greek city councillors to pass on a city that was more beautiful than the one they had taken over. There is a long way to go before such an attribute asserts itself in India (and elsewhere).

# 25

## The Do's and Don'ts of Risk Reduction

The most effective disaster mitigation measure that can be taken at community level is for people not to build in high-risk areas such as unstable slopes, riverbeds or flood plains.

Local knowledge about these hazards is usually good, especially among older people. Sometimes though, a hazard such as a geological fault is not obvious or visible, and surveyors and geologists have to be called in.

People can also ensure they reduce risks in their houses. Roofs should be secured against hurricanes. Roof shape is important for wind resistance. A flat roof is much more likely to be blown off than a pyramid-shaped one. Some worry about the cost of such measures, but they are no more than a small percentage of the total cost of the building and are well worth the investment.

Earthquake mitigation focuses on building codes, including correct use of steel and the strength of concrete mixes. Wooden buildings can be reinforced by braces and tying corners so as to make the structure react as a box.

Hazards in the home are not all structural. If you live in an earthquake-prone area, you should check the following:

- Are heavy objects like cabinets, TV stands and entertainment centres attached to the wall?
- Are heavy objects on the lowest shelves?
- Are water heaters and gas cylinders bolted to the wall?

- Do household members know how to turn off the gas, electricity and water supply?
- Are hanging objects such as fans and ceiling lights securely fastened?
- Are shelves fitted with wire or board to prevent objects falling off them during tremors?
- Are dangerous substances like fuel, poisons and chemical secured against spillage?
- Are plate-glass windows and doors covered with safety film to prevent shattering?

At the national level, government should include mitigation in their disaster management policies. Zoning and land use laws should ensure there are no buildings in an area likely to be flooded, say, once every thirty years. Golf courses and parks could be built there instead. Steep slopes would be left as wooded areas.

But planners and policy maker do not usually have this freedom. Many rivers already flow through towns, so mitigation will take the form of reducing loss of life and damage after a flood. Ground floors can be designated non-sleeping areas, levees can be built and flood warning systems and evacuation plans can be developed.

Building codes should be drafted and where they already exist, should be reviewed and strengthened. They should ensure that buildings can survive a 7 magnitude earthquake or 200 km/h winds.

## Standards of Safety

Many buildings were put up before codes were drafted, so they need to be "retrofitted" by strengthening. This is more expensive than building to resistant standards. Large public buildings and bridges are prime candidates for retrofitting. But small traditional buildings should be strengthened too. Much work has been done on this in India. Chicken mesh and mortar has been effective in reinforcing walls of adobe-type buildings against earthquake damage.

Emergency facilities such as hospitals, police stations and shelters, along with water, electricity and sewage systems, must also be able to remain functional after a disaster. They should be designed to a higher standard of safety than other buildings and retrofitted where necessary. This especially applies to hospitals—crucial after a disaster—as they can be knocked out of actions without structural damage. So non-structural mitigation measures are vital.

Cost is one of the reasons cited for lack of mitigation measures in poor countries. But one could say that such countries cannot afford not to take measures. Even reducing direct damage by one per cent through mitigation would have been worthwhile. But political support for mitigation is hard to drum up because little work has been done on quantifying the benefits of mitigation as opposed to cost.

Mitigation is also very important in the natural environment. Action taken in watersheds in the mountains will eventually affect the marine environment, especially in small countries where the distance between watershed and sea is small. Eroded soil washing down into the ocean results in silting which kills off coral and fish. Coral reefs help control beach and coastal erosion, and if they are damaged the coast is more vulnerable to flooding which will in turn cause more erosion. Coral reefs are also important fish hatching grounds, so loss of reefs will harm the fishing industry, especially in island states. Destruction of reefs and beaches also harms countries, which live off tourism. Chemical spills into waterways eventually reach the sea and also damage coral reefs and marine life. Damaged or stressed reefs are more vulnerable to natural hazards because they are less resistant to wave action.

Dialogue between environmental and disaster managers is essential. For mitigation to work, the entire society must be involved. Programmes should ensure local communities take part in planning at the same time as they ensure political and financial support at national and international level. Mitigation must be part of our daily life. If the present century "invented" mitigation and moved disaster management beyond mere response, the next must see that mitigation becomes an integral part of planning at all levels of society.

# 26

## Safety First

Throughout history, the violent side of nature has manifested itself in destructive phenomena such as floods, volcanic eruptions, severe storms, wildfires, earthquakes and tidal waves. Disasters and risks are part of our life, and they will continue to threaten, kill and destroy. "Zero risk" is out of reach in the contemporary world. The basic problem is how to prevent hazards from causing increasingly large-scale disasters. The answer is that the disastrous effects of natural phenomena will only be eliminated, reduced or stabilized when people decide to make cities, settlements, infrastructures and houses safer.

### A Culture of Prevention

For people are the agents of disaster. "It's not the bullet that kills, it's the hole". Earthquakes and windstorms do not kill, the collapse of houses and buildings from shaking is the main cause of death. Natural hazards themselves are not on the increase; nor are they likely to be in the future. It is the frequency of natural disasters that is expected to grow, as well as their complexity, scope, gravity and destructive capacity there will be an increase in multiple or synergistic-type disasters causing society-wide impacts. In a time of globalisation, largescale damage caused by an earthquake in a world financial centre is bound to have an effect even on the economies of far-away countries.

Natural disasters are not always entirely "natural". On the one hand, natural forces are at work on planet whose environment is being altered day after day by humankind: floods are made moreover by deforestation, global warming more preoccupying by the unchecked emission of greenhouse gases. On the other, natural disasters will increasingly generate or magnify concurrent technological disasters. Floods can devastate chemical complexes, earthquakes can affect critical plants.

The good news is that diaster reduction is both possible and feasible. While we cannot prevent an earthquake or a windstorm from occurring, or a volcano from erupting, we can use the scientific knowledge and technical know-how that we already have in order to increase the earthquake—and wind-resistance of houses and bridges, and to issue and disseminate early warnings of volcanic eruptions and organise proper community response to such warnings. The extent to which society puts this knowledge to effective use depends upon its social, cultural, political, economic, and even religious specificities.

## Informing the Public

Disaster prevention and preparedness start with improving our understanding of risks by assessing the distribution in time and space and the intensity of the natural phenomena involved and the exposure of people and structures to them. On the basis of this assessment, protective measures may be taken such as land-use restrictions, adequate construction measures and wise environmental management. Detection and warning systems may be installed, and contingency and emergency plans be set up. One permanent measure of paramount importance is the education and information of the public.

A number of cases show that loss of life, injuries and physical damage can all be significantly reduced by the application of better warning and disaster prevention measures. Because of inadequate use of, and response to, warning, more than 300,000 people died in Bangladesh due to a cyclone in November 1970. In May 1985, better prediction and proper response to warning of a cyclone of the same intensity kept the death toll below 10,000. Similarly, appropriate warning and evacuation saved the people in India in various cyclones.

Disaster prevention measures cost much less than relief and reconstruction expenditure following a disaster, yet many decision-makers tend to focus on relief and to treat disaster situations in an ad hoc way when they are presented with them. Today most typical strategies are crisis-oriented. Furthermore, information about natural hazards and disaster reduction techniques is not well disseminated, and planners, project managers and communities do not integrate hazard management into development planning. Resources spent on relief and recovery continue to account for 96 per cent of all resources spent on disaster-related activities annually, leaving a pitiful 4 per cent for disaster prevention. It is high time to make a shift in emphasis from post-disaster reaction to pre-disaster action.

# 27

# The Nature and Causes of Drug Addiction

Man has been experimenting for thousands of years with a variety of naturally occurring substances that act on his nervous tissues: alcohol to intoxicate a weary mind, belladonna to calm an angry intestine or to poision an adversary, opium to overcome worry and strain. The relief of pain, in particular, in an age-old aim of mankind, and various narcotic and sleep-producing agents were probably used by primitive man. But for many men there is another kind of pain the pain of being—and from time immemorial some men have been trying to expand their vision, enhance their appreciation of their world, change their mood, alter their inner existence, or stupefy their awareness with such drugs as alcohol, opium, and cannabis.

Drugs, chemical substances that affect the functions of living things, are used in treating, preventing and diagnosing diseases. The most important source of drugs today is chemical synthesis. The increase in the manufacture of drugs has resulted in the development of 25,000 or more drugs and drugs products. Many drugs are potentially dangerous chemicals that can cause serious, sometimes fatal, poisoning if used incorrectly: governments of various countries, therefore, have established certain legal requirements concerning drug use.

**Uses:** The main purpose of the use of drugs is to cure disease or correct a disorder. Chemotherapeutic drugs, such as the antibiotics, the sulfa drugs, and the antimalarial drugs, flight infection by acting directly on disease causing invading organisms, either immobilizing or killing them. Some chemotherapeutic drugs are also used to suppress or prevent infection.

**Drug Toxicity**

No drug is free of toxic effects. This factor is what ultimately limits the usefulness of drugs. Some of the untoward effects of drugs are trivial and can be readily tolerated. Others, however, are serious and may even be fatal. Some toxic effects of drug are merely extension of the drug's therapeutic effects.

This is why drugs never should be taken except under the guidance of a physican. A physician is aware of the potential hazards of a drug and is prepared to act promptly if toxicity occurs. Furthermore, the physician is aware that many of the toxic effects produced by drugs are unexpected, bizarre, and often not clearly related to the taking of a drug.

Many people suffer from drug allergy—one of the most serious problems of pharmacology. Penicillin, for example, is an extremely safe drug for most people, but it produces hypersensitivity reactions in about 15% of the population. In some cases the reaction is so serious that is necessary to forbid the future use of penicillin because of the risk of death. Drug allergy takes many different forms; skin reactions varying from a mild rash to severe dermatitis.

**Drug Addiction and Abuse.** It is a very likely that every society has had mood-changing drug and that there have always been individuals who used them in ways that were not socially approved. In this sense, drug abuse, the socially nonsanctioned use of a drug, is universal and so old a history. Which behaviours are called drug abuse varies from culture to culture and from time to time within the same culture. Since laws do not always correspond to prevalent social attitudes, there may be times when users of an illegal drug are not considered to be drug abusers. Form a pharmacological viewpoint, attitudes toward drugs are often inconsistent or irrational. Some drugs may be totally outlawed, while others with similar actions are made generally available and may be self-administered with full social approval.

The repeated use of some drugs can lead be a dependence on the drug, in which the effects of the drug or the conditions associated with its use are felt by the users to be necessary for their well being. Dependence may vary in intensity from a mild inclination to a strong craving or compulsion to use the drug. Severe dependence may result in a type of behaviour is also known as Compulsive drug use, and since a severe dependence on any self-administered drug is generally not socially approved, the term is usually synonymous with compulsive drug abuse. One obvious exception is the use of tobacco, where social acceptance is so complete that even heavy compulsive use which is damaging to the user's health, is commonly not considered to be drug abuse.

The term drug has been defined in many ways, but in this article it is used to mean a behavioural pattern of compulsive drug use characterized by an overwhelming involvement with the procurement and use of the drug and the high tendency of the user to relapse to drug use after a period of abstinence. It is synonymous with intensive or severe drug dependence. Contrary to popular belief, drug addiction is not same as physical dependence on a drug. Physical dependence is a physiological or biochemical condition produced by the administration of a drug to the extent that a characteristic pattern of signs and symptoms appears when the drug is withdrawn and disappears when the drug is administered again. Physical dependence can be produced by a wide variety of drugs that are used in everyday medical practice. Some drugs that produce physical dependence are not pleasant to take and are neither abused nor used compulsively. Also, not all withdrawal symptoms are associated with a craving for the drug that produced the physical dependence.

**The Nature and Causes of Drug Addiction**

If opium were the only drug of abuse, and the only kind of abuse were one of habitual, compulsive use, discussion of addiction might be a simple matter. But opium is not the only drug of abuse, and there are probably as many kinds of abuse as there are drugs to abuse, or indeed, as may be there are persons who abuse. Various substances are used in so many different ways by so many different or one definition could possibly embrace all the medical, psychiatric, psychological, sociological, cultural, economic, religious, ethical, and legal considerations that have an important bearing on addiction. Prejudice and ignorance have led to the labeling of all use of nonsanctioned drugs as addiction and of all drugs, when misused, as narcotics. The continued practice of treating addiction as a single entity is dictated by custom and law, not by the facts of addiction.

Many substances are capable of acting on biological systems, and whether a particular substance comes to be considered a drug depends, in large measure, upon whether it is capable of eliciting a "drug like" effect that is valued by the user. There is nothing intrinsic to the substances themselves that sets one active substance is imparted to it by use. Caffeine, nicotine, and alcohol are clearly drugs, and the habitual excessive use of coffee, if not addiction. The same could be extended to cover tea, chocolates, or powdered sugar, if society wished to use and consider them that way. The task of defining addiction, then is the task of being able to distinguish between opium and powdered sugar while at the same time being able to embrace the fact that both can be subject to abuse. This requires a frame of reference that recognizes that almost any substance can be considered a drug, that almost any drug is capable of abuse, that one kind of abuse may differ appreciably from another kind of abuse, and that the effect valued by the user will differ from one individual to the next for a particular drug, or from one drug to the next drug for a particular individual. This kind of reference would still leave unanswered various questions of availability, public sanction, and one kind of effect rather than another at a particular moment in history, but it does at least acknowledge that drug addiction is not a unitary condition.

**Effect on the Mind and Body.** The effects of drugs similar in may ways to those of alcohol. Low doses usually produce relaxation and decreases anxiety; higher doses produce drowsiness. Even if people can stay awake, they may appear confused and show poor judgement and loss of emotional control. Slurred speech, a staggering gait, muscular incoordination and nystagmus (rapid involuntary eye movements) are also characteristic effects. Although alcohol and the sedative-hypnotics are all depressants of the nervous system, low or moderate doses can produce an effect that resembles stimulation. The individual may become euphoric and more active, and show a decrease in inhibitions. Very high doses produce coma and death due to respiratory failure.

**Drugs In Psychiatry.** Drugs that are used either alone or in conjunction with psychotherapy to treat psychiatric illness. The medical treatment of psychiatric illness is based on a firm conviction that the patient's behaviour is in fact a symptom of an illness and not simply a variant of acceptable behaviour in society. The study of drug effects on mental processes is called psychopharmacology.

Certain patterns of disease with mental manifestations are biologically characteristic of humans. The use of drugs to treat these disease patterns is directed either at alleviating symptoms or at inhibiting or stopping the underlying disease processes. Diseases that have purely psychological causes, but appear in ways that disturb society or distress the individual, are often treated with nonspecific remedies, that either sedate or alert the individual. For all mental illness with specific biological causes, psychopharmacologists seek to develop drugs that change the biological functioning of the individual so that the symptoms of disease either do not occur or have a lesser impact on his or her life and behaviour.

The use of drugs in the treatment of psychiatric illness is not a denial of the importance of psychological or social factors in the causation or pattern of a disease. Drug treatment of psychiatric illness is based on the principle that the human nervous system is always a chemical biological system. Some psychiatric treatment system—for example, psychoanalysis—do not utilize drug treatment. Some mental health experts feel that the use of drugs is only for the control of patients and not their treatment.

## Social and Ethical Issues of Drug Use

### *Conflicting Values in Drug Use*

The social and economic requirements of modern society may have undergone a radical change in the last few decades, even though the inertia of the existing social character, its desires and its values, will be felt for some time to come. In one major sense, current drug controversies are a reflection of this cultural lag with all of the consequent conflict of wished and values that result of the consequent conflict of wishes and values that result from the lack of good correspondence between traditional teachings and the view of the world as it is now being perceived by large numbers within society. Modern society is in a state of rapid transition, and this transition is not without its untoward consequences in terms of stability.

Cultural transitions notwithstanding, the dominant social order has strong negative feelings about any nonsanctioned use of drugs that contradicts its existing value system. Can society succeed if individuals are allowed unrestrained self-indulgence? Is it bad to rely on something so much that one cannot exist without it? Is it legitimate to take drugs if one is not sick? Does one have right to decide for oneself what one needs? Does society have the right to punish someone if he has done no harm to himself or to others? These are difficult questions that do not admit to ready answers. Once can guess what the answers would be to the nonsanctioned use of drugs. The traditional ethic dictates harsh responses to conduct that is "self-indulgent" or "abusive of pleasure." But how does one account for the quantities of the drugs being manufactured and consumed today by the general public? It is one thing to talk of the few hundred thousand or so "hard" narcotic users who are principally addicted to the opiates. One might still feel comfortable in disparaging the widespread illicit use of hallucinogenic substances: these are still the "other guys". But the sedatives, tranquilizers, sleeping remedies, stimulants, alcohol, coffee, tea, and tobacco are complications that trap the advocate in some glaring inconsistencies. It may be asked by partisans whether the cosmetic use of stimulants for weight control is any more legitimate than the use of stimulants to "get with it?"; whether the conflict-ridden businessman or the conflict-ridden housewife is any more entitled to relax chemically (alcohol, tranquilizers, sleeping aids, sedatives) than the conflict-ridden adolescent?"; Whether physical pain is any less bearable than mental pain or anguish? Billions of pills and capsules of a nonnarcotic type are manufactured yearly.

Sedatives and tranquilizers account for somewhere around 12 to 20 per cent of all doctor's prescriptions. In addition there are about 150 different sleeping aids that are available for sale without a prescription. The alcoholic beverage industry produces countless millions of gallons of wine and spirits and countless millions of barrels of beer each year. One might conclude that there is a whole drug culture; that the problem is not confined to the young, the poor, the disadvantaged, or even to the criminal' that existing attitudes are at least inconsistent, possibly hypocritical. One always justifies one's own drug use, but one tends to view the other fellow who uses the same drugs as an abuser who is weak and undesirable. It must be recognized that the social consensus is regard to drug use and abuse is limited, conflict ridden, and often glaringly inconsistent. The problem is not one of insufficient facts but one of multiple objectives that at the present moment appear unreconcilable.

# 28

# Population Growth and Natural Recreation Areas

Population growth during the past 50 years has made it difficult to set aside and conserve natural areas. Another half century of growth will put even more pressure on protected area as formerly small, distant settlements encroach on these sites and as the number of people (both local and visitors) who use these sites explodes.

National parks, forests, wildlife preserves, beaches, and other protected areas offer sanctuary to various habitats and indigenous communities, in addition to providing resources for local peoples. In an urbanizing world, these sites provide an opportunity for healthy interaction with the natural environment, as well as rare serenity.

From Buenos Aires to Bangkok, dramatic population growth in the world's major cities and the sprawl and pollution they bring—threatens natural recreation areas that lay beyond city limits. Tremendous growth in the population of Bombay has already engulfed Borivili National Park, a reserve that was boyond the city's periphery only a decade ago. With projected growth of 60 per cent in the next 20 years, Bombay may soon swallow up more distant areas. On every continent, human encroachment has reduced both the size and the quality of national recreation areas.

In nations where rapid population growth has outstripped the carrying capacity of local resources, protected area become especially vulnerable. Although in industrial nations these areas are synonymous with camping, hiking, and picnics in the country, in Asia, Africa and Latin America most national parks, forests, and preserves are inhabited or used for natural resources by local populations.

An assessment by the World Conservation Union-IUCN of 30 protected sites in the developing world shows that these areas now act as magnets, attracting people to the rich oasis of water, fuel, food, and other resources they contain. Population growth rates in and around these areas are typically 2 percentage points above the national average—largely as a result of immigration from resource-starved areas.

As people seek out scarce resources, the resulting concentrations can be devastating. For example, population densities in the region surrounding Bwindi Impenetrable National Park in southern Uganda are some of the highest in all of Africa—exceeding 250 people for square kilometer. Though population at this site is expected to multiply, chronic land hunger already precipitates conflicts over fuel-wood collection, farming, cattle grazing, and bush burning.

Migration-driven population growth also endangers natural recreation areas in many industrial nations. Everglades National Park faces collapse as millions of new-comers move into South Florida.

Coastal recreation areas, including beaches, may be most burdened by the formidable combination of population growth and migration. All but one of the world's 15 largest cities—Mexico City—are coastal, and all of these cities will grow in the decades ahead. Whether it takes the form of expanding shantytowns in Kingston, Jamaica, or sprawling tract housing in southern California, virtually all the growth and movement in population in the next 50 years will occur in densely populated coastal corridors.

In nations already struggling to meet basic human needs, the prospect of establishing additional protected areas becomes increasingly slim. Throughout India, for example, while the national government designates areas as protected, state and local governments work to de-reserve these sites so that the resources can be harnessed to meet the needs of an additional 18 million Indians each year.

Sunbathers on beaches in Japan are often compared to sardines. People who use Central Park in New York City, which has nearly doubled in population since 1950, are faced with growing congestion and restrictions on activities. National parks throughout North America are confronted with huge backlogs of requests to visit, having to turn tourists away. Tourism at Yosemite has boomed from roughly 4,000 visitors in 1886 to more than 4 million people (and their cars) today. In is often remarked that "Americans love their national parks to death", as increased visitation degrades campsites, trails, and wilderness.

Longer waiting lists and higher user fees for fewer secluded spots are likely the tip of the iceberg, as population growth threatens to eliminate the diversity of habitats and cultures, in addition to the space and quiet, that protected areas currently house.

# 29

# Pollution for Export

After tax havens ... pollution havens? Are multinationals seeking to relocate in countries with low environmental standards? It all depends on how you look at it. In the search for new sources of capital, labour and raw materials are multinational corporations looking to relocate in "pollution havens" where environmental regulations are lax if not non-existent?

The question is increasingly being asked at a time when the level of foreign direct investment (FDI) is rising sharply. This is mainly due to the fact that both "source" and "host" countries recognize that each have something to gain from the FDI process. However, some observers are afraid that economic gains are being generated at the expense of environmental quality and other important elements of social welfare. They worry that "host" countries will compete for the benefits of new FDI by lowering their environmental standards or by reducing efforts to enforce existing standards, and that firms will relocate to these "pollution havens", to gain a cost advantage over their competitors. In this scenario, developing countries are regarded as the most likely sites of pollution havens because they may be the countries most willing to trade off their environmental quality for economic gains, and industrialized countries are cast in the role of predators willing to degrade the environment of developing countries in order to generate economic gains for themselves. However, most research suggests that, overall, companies do not invest overseas to obtain access to lower environmental costs.

It is difficult to determine whether FDI flows are affected by the level of environmental regulations existing in foreign countries. Foreign capital clearly flows to a wide range of countries, industries and companies some of which are careful environmental stewards, some of which are not. A firm may in any case invest in a country to take advantage of a high quality labour force and other factors unrelated to environmental costs.

## Respect for the Environment: A Good Selling Point

Environmental costs are often a relatively small component of total production costs, which may sometimes even be lower when environmental standards are higher (for example, where lower environmental standards lead to higher costs of treating industrial water supplies).

Multinationals often seem more interested in consistent enforcement of environmental rules than in lower standards per se. Moreover, companies are often willing to make new investments that actually improve the environment, so long as their main competitors are also required to do so. Part of the reason for this is that multinational frequently apply a single environmental standard to their world-wide operations, regardless of any (lower) standards which may exist in a particular country. There could be three main reasons for this.

First, the firm may have calculated that it cannot afford to see the reputation of its products in the (global) market-place tarnished by charges of "environmental exploitation" in one particular location-charges which can sometimes result in boycotts or other forms of consumer pressure. For example, investors in Puerto Rican banana production firms have insisted on "due environmental care" by those firms, because they perceive that overseas markets for their products will demand higher levels of environmental quality.

Second, the firm may have calculated that it is less expensive to apply a single environmental standard to its (globally integrated) production processes, rather than to develop 'tailor-made" production lines, based on varying levels of environmental standards.

Finally, the ability of firms to make "dirty" investments may be limited by requirements in their home country. For example, the US Ex-Im Bank requires any US company taking advantage of its export financing assistance to meet certain minimum environmental criteria.

On the other hand, there is some evidence to suggest that "pollution havens" do exist within certain types of firms, operating in specific industries, and in particular countries. Investments made in the resource extraction and processing sectors, such as chemicals, metallurgy, logging, and pulp and paper, fall into this category. In these industries, pollution control costs can make up a significant proportion of the firm's total costs. The result can be that small cost differences can translate into large changes in market share and profitability. These firms are more susceptible to the level of environmental costs, and therefore more likely to invest in "pollution havens". However, this does not necessarily mean that countries actually lower their environmental standards to attract new investments.

There is clearly competition, both within and between countries, to obtain access to new FDI. It is particularly keen in the rapidly-industrializing countries, and in countries which are dependent on the resource extraction and processing industries in which the potential for hard currency export earnings may be very high. In these situations, incoming investors can often successfully argue for relief from "high" environmental costs.

But surprising though it may seem, investors in resource-based industries do not always exert pressures for lower environmental standards-sometimes they may even want standards in the host country to be raised.

Competitive pressures can also translate into a desire to reduce waste and improve productivity, which can lead to improved environmental performance. An ethic of eco-efficiency, which seeks to "design out" pollution problems rather than deal with unwanted waste, is increasingly accepted.

FDI is also often associated with modern technologies which represent environmental improvements over what is currently available in the host country. Once the investment has been made, local firms may try to imitate multinationals' environmental practices. But there is also evidence that certain kinds of enterprises (e.g. the town and village enterprises of rural China) seem prone to use outdated technical equipment from other countries that does not represent the "best environmental technology", because they are undercapitalized and because this equipment is cheap.

There is also some evidence that "pollution havens" may be associated with something other than the level of environmental standards. For example, pollution intensities did appear to increase more rapidly in Latin America as a whole between 1970 and 1990, after environmental regulations in OECD countries became stricter. But it was not the countries with the lowest environmental standards which attracted the most pollution intensive investment it was those countries which were less open to FDI in the first place. "Pollution havens" were found, but they seemed to be more closely associated with protectionist economies than with lower environmental standards.

Overall, countries which operate straight forward, transparent, and efficient environmental programmes seem to experience no particular loss of FDI flows, and may in fact attract some industries which are looking for reliable overseas bases of operation. In short, governments are recognizing that lowering environmental standards to attract new FDI is often unnecessary.

# 30

## Ecosystems, Our Unknown Protectors

How ecosystems work and what part they play in biodiversity remain a mystery. But we do know that they perform a host of invaluable services for the human species. In my view, biodiversity's fundamental value is neither aesthetic nor economic but environmental, even though most people are largely unaware of this. The value of biodiversity is often measured in terms of the number of species living in a given area. But the interactions between the many species in an ecosystem, and between them and the environment's physical and chemical components are also very important. This highly intricate web of relationships makes an ecosystem more valuable than the su:r of the species it contains.

Ecosystems perform services that are essential for the survival of the human species. They fix carbon in the atmosphere and produce oxygen, protect soil from erosion and keep it fertile, filter water and replenish aquifers, provide pollination and anti-parasite agents and so on.

The first two of these services are closely related to each other. They result from photosynthesis, whereby green plants, starting with algae, absorb carbon dioxide ($CO_2$) and emit oxygen. For millions for years, the balance between the various gases in the atmosphere remained stable. But with the coming of the industrial revolution, humans began burning increase amounts of fossil fuels. Today, three billion tonnes of carbon build up in the atmosphere each year and natural ecosystems can no longer absorb all these emissions—especially since they are disappearing at an alarming rate. Deforestation alone releases such tremendous amounts of $CO_2$ and other gases, such as methane, that it has become the second-leading cause of global warning.

Strong freshwater, protecting soil and keeping it fertile are three other closely related functions. Ecosystems are veritable "freshwater factories". They absorb rainwater and slowly filter it through the soil before draining it towards streams, rivers, lakes and underground aquifers that supply us with the precious liquid. When the vegetal ground cover is degraded, the water cycle is disrupted. Rain strikes the bare earth, washing away huge amounts of nutritional substances. Reservoirs, lakes and rivers silt up.

## Uncertain Reaction to Climate Change

Despite years of research, scientists still know very little about how ecosystems work. We are generally incapable of predicting how they will react to certain transformations in the environment, especially climate changes. Nor do we know any more about whether a species present in a given environment is superfluous or "replicate", even when it is very rare. Likewise, we do not know which key species are indispensable to maintaining an ecosystem, with a few exceptions such as pine forests, where that tree is obviously the dominant species.

We know even less about the part biological diversity itself play in maintaining ecosystems and the services they perform. One simple example is a highest diversified forest that absorbs carbon dioxide—a vital function, as we have seen, for limiting global warming. Suppose the forest is cleared to make way for a single-crop forest. The service will still be performed, perhaps even better at first because young, fast-growing trees absorb more $CO_2$ than old ones, which regenerate slowly. But what will happen in the long term? After several decades, the consequences of the loss of biodiversity will probably be felt. Replacing many species with a single one will have certainly depleted the soil and, in the long term, slowed down the forest's growth and consequently its ability to absorb $CO_2$.

More generally, diversified ecosystems seem more productive. Specialists remain wary about their conclusions, but today they believe that biodiversity helps ecosystems to resist alien species and diseases and to recover faster in the event of disruption. In the face of doubt, and to find out more about them, it is better to preserve as many different ecosystems as possible.

**A Costly Lesson for New York City**

Most people take it for granted that ecosystems will carry on performing services without receiving anything in return. They think nature will continue benefiting humanity, no matter how much damage is done. The survival of organisms other than our own species is perceived as a frill that future generations can live without.

These preconceived ideas are wrong and dangerous as the city of New York has recently come to realize. The city's water has always enjoyed such a good reputation that it was sold throughout the northeastern United States. Its equality was due to Catskill Mountains' natural purification system. But that ecosystem has suffered so much from pollution, especially fertilizer run-off from farms, that by the late 1990s New York's water had become undrinkable. The city planned to build a purification plant, whose cost was put at between six and eight billion dollars, not including the $300 million in yearly operating costs—an astronomical bill for a service that had always been free! The price was so staggering that the city eventually decided to restore the Catskill Mountains' degraded environment at a cost of only one billion dollars.

This story clearly illustrates where our interests lie. We must preserve ecosystems and the conditions that enable our planet to ensure the survival of *Homo sapiens* or, at least, the short-term maintenance of our current quality of life.

# 31

## Forests:

### *The Earth's Lungs*

The world's forest cover is shrinking. Over the past 50 years nearly half of the world's original forest cover has been lost—some 3 billion hectares. Each year another 16 million hectares of virgin forest are cut, bulldozed, or burned.

Between 1980 and 1995 the world lost some 180 million hectares of forest—an area the size of Indonesia. While developed countries had a net increase of 20 million hectares due to reforestation, this gain was more than offset by a net decrease of 200 million hectares in the developing world.

Forests have many functions of value both to humanity and to nature itself. Take away the trees, and the intricately linked ecosystem unravels. Forests absorb carbon dioxide and produce oxygen, anchor soils, regulate the water cycle, protect against erosion, and provide a habitat for millions of species.

Forests products are essential to the world economy, worth about US$400 billion annually in timber, pulp, paper, and fuel wood. Forest products other than wood, such as medicines, vegetables, and fruits, provide another US$20 billion and are growing in importance.

Healthy forests boost food production. Trees soak up and store water from season to season, slowly releasing moisture during dry periods. Without tree cover, water runs off faster during the tropical rainy season, carrying away valuable topsoil. A World Bank study found that the rate of soil loss was 10 times higher on forest lands where slash-and-burn shifting cultivation was practiced than in undisturbed forests.

One reason that agricultural yields have fallen in sub Sahran Africa is that vast amounts of forests cover have disappeared, hastening soil erosion and loss of soil nutrients.

Forest cover regulates climate, while destruction of forests contribute to global warning. Whereas living trees soak up and store carbon dioxide from the atmosphere trees that are cut down and burned release carbon into the atmosphere. In the last decade tropical deforestation has released large amounts of stored carbon—accounting for roughly one-quarter of the carbon dioxide emissions to the atmosphere due to human activity.

**Pressures on Forests**

Current demand for forests products may exceed the limits of sustainable consumption by 25%. The developed world accounts for most of the demand for forest products. With just 16% of the world's population, North America, Europe, and Japan consume two-thirds of the world's paper and paperboard and half its industrial wood. Demand for industrial wood products also has risen in developing countries, however, along with demand for fuel wood, the main energy source for many rural communities.

Throughout the 1990s many developing countries with rapid population growth had high rates of deforestation. Forest land was converted to agricultural use, and trees cut to provide housing and wood for fuel. Moreover developing countries steeped up exports of forests, products to meet the rising demand from developed countries.

The amount of forest area per capita fell by half between 1960 and 1995 reflecting both population growth and the disappearance of forests cover. In 1995 close to 1.7 billion people lived in countries with less than one-tenth of a hectare of forest cover per capita (83). By 2025, an estimated 4.6 billion people will live in such countries.

**What Can Be Done?**

As population grows and per capita consumption of forest products increases, countries must do more to manage forest resources on a sustainable basis. The following developments offer encouragement:

### Technological Improvements

Technological improvements including use of recycled paper and paperboard, have substantially reduced the amount of pulp needed to produce paper. In 1970 paper and paperboard consisted of 80% wood pulp. By 1997 more efficient production processes had reduced that figure to 56%. As a direct result, the production of pulp for paper is expected to grow by just over 1% a year over the next decade, about half the growth rate in the 1980s.

### Forest Products Certification

Adopting a system that identifies forest products that come from sustainable managed forests could support efforts toward sustainability. As of 1998, about 10 million hectares of forest lands have been certified. Over 90% of the certified area is in northern, temperature forests, mostly in Europe and North America. Close to 60% of the entire certified area is in just two countries—Sweden and Poland—reflecting education and awareness campaigns in those countries. In tropical forests, where most of the destruction is taking place today, only tiny areas have been certified as providing sustainable yield.

### Intergovernmental Responses

In 1995 the Intergovernmental Panel on forests (IPF) was established in response to the 1992 Earth Summit. The IPF evolved into the inter governmental Forum on Forests in 1997, after the UN's five year review of the Earth Summit goals. The mission of the forum is to examine the underlying causes of deforestation and to help countries develop strategies that address them.

Efforts to advance an international legal convention on forests, which began in 1990, have been shelved, however. Some observers believe that advancing such a convention would only codify the standards of a weak consensus and thus would be worse than no convention at all. Widespread opposition to a convention makes it unlikely that the issues will reach the negotiating table.

Instead, many organisations urge governments of countries with large forest resources to enforce existing legislation and to introduce more effective forest conservation initiatives close to 130 countries have developed or updated their National Forest programmes over the past decade.

While such initiatives are promising, they cannot be expected to half forest destruction completely. Millions of people rely on forest products for their livelihoods. Sustainable forest management will require not just enforcement of laws that project forests but also alternative sources of livelihood for many rural people.

# Bibliography


Anand, R.P., *Legal Regime of Sea Bed and the Developing Countries*, 1975.

Bhatt, S., *Environment Protection and International Law*, Radiant Pulication, Kalkaji, New Delhi, 1985, pp.122.

Bhatt, S., *Environmental Laws and Water Resources Management*, Radiant Publication, India, and Advent Books Inc. New York, 1986, pp. 355.

Behrman, Danial, *In partnership with Nature-UNESCO and the Environment* (Paris, 1973).

Bell, Daniel, "Technology, Nature and Society", *American Scholar*, Summer 1973.

Bentley, Glass, "Biology and Human Values", USIS, New Delhi.

*Book of Nature: The Way Things* Work, published by George Allen and Unwin Ltd., 1981, pp. 525.

Boulding, Kenneth E., "New Goals for Society", S.H. Schun, ed., *Energy, Economic Growth and the Environment.*

Carr, E.H., *What is History*, 1961.

Darlington, C.D., *The Evolution of Man and Society* (London, 1961).

Downing, Paul B., ed., *Air Pollution and Social Sciences* (New York 1971)

"Drive to adopt national water policy", *Time of India*, 22 July, 1983.

Dubos, Rene, "Man and his Environment", *Britannica Perspectives*, vol. 1, 1968.

Einstein, A., *My Views*, ed. by S.K. Bandopadhyaya (Calcutta, 1976).

"Environment Research Programme", prepared by NCEPC, Department of Science and Technology, New Delhi.

Forbes, R.J., "The Conqest of Nature and its Consequences", *Britannica Perspective*, vol. 1, 1968.

Fowler, John M., *Energy and Environment* (New York, 1975).

Fuller, Buckminister R., *Operating Manual for Spaceship Earth* (New York, 1969).

Gandhi, Indira, "Poverty Greatest Polloution, says Mrs Gandhi", *Time of of India,* 8 September, 1981.

Glenn, Seaborg, "Science, Technology and Development: A New World Outlook", USIS, New Delhi.

Hacoley, Amos H., *Human Ecology* (New York, 1950).

"India must develop own ecology", *Times of India,* 8 October.1981.

Marion, Jerry B., *Energy in Perspective* (London,1974)

Misra, K.C., *Manual of Plant Ecology,* New Delhi, 1980.

Mukherji, P.K., *Life of Tagore,* trans, by S.K. Ghosh, 1975.

Mumford, Lewis, "The Future of Cities", in *Basic Issues in Environment,* E.J. Winn, ed., 1972.

Palmslierna, H., *Future Imperatives for Human Enivronment,* 1972.

Pavithran, A.K., "World Futurology", *Eastern Journal of International Law* (Madras), vol. 9.

"Plans to usher Indiá into 21st Century," *Time of India,* 24 October, 1985.

Polunin, Nicholas, "The Biosphere Today", *The Environmental Future,* Proceedings of 1st International Conference on Environmental Future in Finland, ed. by N. Polunin, 1972.

Radhakrishnan, S., *Recovery of Faith,* 1967.

*Report on the State of Environment* Prepared by Centre for Science and Environment, New Delhi, 1985.

Sarkar, Mahendra Nath, *The Cultural Heritage of India,* vol. 1.

Sen, Sudhir, "Blueprint for a better World", *Time of India,* 2 March, 1980.

*The Limits to Growth,* a report to Club of Rome (New York, 1972).

*The Mind of J. Krishnamurti,* ed. by L.S.R. Vas (Bombay, 1971).

Toynbee, Arnold. "Man and his Soul," *Hindustan Times,* 4 January, 1968.

*United Nations List of National Parks and Protected Areas,* 1985.

Vivekananda, Swami, *Complete Works,* vol II (Calcutta, 1968)

Ward, Barbara and Dubos Rene, *Only one Earth: The Care and maintenance of a small planet,* Report to UN Conference on human environment, Stockholm, 1972.

"Wildlife laws in India", *Times of India,* 4 March, 1985.

Ward, Barbara, *Progress for a Small Planet,* 1979.

# Index

**F**



**G**



**H**